Penguin Handbooks

Quick Cook

Beryl Downing is a journalist whose interest in
cooking was stimulated as a child by an inventive
Swiss mother and a sailor father who brought back
food and traveller's tales from all over the world.
On her own travels in Europe and America she
has collected many interesting recipes which she
has adapted to fit in with the combination of family
and full-time career which is the dual role of many
modern women.

She was the Quick Cook for the London *Evening
News* for four years, before becoming the shopping
editor for *The Times*, and it is her firm belief that
the main qualification of a good, self-taught cook
is a willingness to taste anything once.

Beryl Downing

QUICK COOK

*Recipes in Thirty Minutes
and Under*

Penguin Books

Penguin Books Ltd, Harmondsworth, Middlesex, England
Penguin Books, 625 Madison Avenue, New York, New York 10022, U.S.A.
Penguin Books Australia Ltd, Ringwood, Victoria, Australia
Penguin Books Canada Ltd, 2801 John Street, Markham, Ontario, Canada L3R 1B4
Penguin Books (N.Z.) Ltd, 182-190 Wairau Road, Auckland 10, New Zealand

First published 1981

Copyright © Beryl Downing, 1981

All rights reserved

Made and printed in Great Britain by
Richard Clay (The Chaucer Press) Ltd,
Bungay, Suffolk
Set in Monotype Bembo

To Steve,
for testing, trying –
and surviving

CONTENTS

INTRODUCTION

This is not an I-hate-cooking book. It's an I-like-it-but-I-haven't-the-time. It began as a daily recipe service called 'Quick Cook' in the London *Evening News*, specially created for commuters who, married, single, old, young, men, women, all travel at least half an hour a day to their offices. After squeezing themselves home in a tube they don't want to spend hours concocting an evening meal. But they don't want to get into a chops-on-Wednesday routine, either. And that applies quite often to people whose work is their home, as well as to those for whom home is too much like hard work.

Of course, there are always times when a special occasion demands a great deal of effort. Some people's special occasions crop up only on high days and holidays, other's once or twice a week. But the rest of the time, the problem is to find quick and interesting ways of serving real food – ready-mades out of a packet are strictly taboo.

So I don't propose to tell you how to improve the shining can by adding a dash of Australian sherry. I do hope to show that, even if you don't have time to plan, and most of your shopping is done at weekends or in lunch hours, it is still possible to produce interesting dishes in half an hour or less.

Nothing in this book takes more than 30 minutes to make from start to finish, including preparation. Some are simple family favourites, some are quick versions of more complicated classics, some are new inventions to tempt the tastebuds and stimulate the imagination. Sometimes there's a bit of cheating – overnight freezing or setting, for instance, in order to add variety and to save time the following day. But dishes like casseroles, which need long cooking, are not included, as they do mean a certain amount of supervision, if only occasionally.

In addition to individual dishes which take from 10 to 30 minutes each, there is a section of menus which shows that you can produce several satisfying two-course family meals and even an instant dinner party – all in half an hour. There is a section for slimmers, too – calorie-counted recipes that can be served to the whole family so that they need never suspect a slimmer in their midst. And there's a chapter on low-cholesterol eating for anyone worried about health. Both slimming and low-cholesterol are big enough subjects for whole books to themselves and if you have been worried by either problem for long, you will no doubt have a specialist book on your shelves already. But many people have weight or health problems for relatively brief periods in their lives, so these chapters are included for them, as an introduction and guide.

It is not my intention to give recipes specifically for freezing, although those which do freeze successfully will be indicated with an [F]. If you are the sort of careful provider who makes fifteen pizzas, six pounds of spaghetti sauce and five casseroles at a time to stash away for an appropriate moment, I imagine you are also well enough organized to remember to get them out in time to defrost, so you don't need advice on that score. But many people have a small freezer section at the top of the fridge and it can be extremely useful to have a home-made soup or ice cream ready to pad out an instant main course into a 30-minute meal. Moreover, plans can change at the last minute and if you have prepared food which is not after all required, it is useful to know when it can be frozen for use another time – hence the [F].

The main purpose of this book, then, is to help you when you haven't had time to plan. For this you need to be flexible, to be able to overcome the tyranny of the meat and two veg, and particularly to learn to substitute no-preparation foods like pasta and rice for the dreaded wash-and-scrub potato routine.

Most vegetables need very little cooking time, but you have to learn which need least pre-cooking attention and at what stage you can fit this in to your main course cooking. You need to unlearn all you ever heard about getting all your ingredients together before you start cooking. As long as you have well-organized cupboards you can save at least 5 minutes of your half hour by getting things out as you need them, rather than assembling them in advance. But get into the habit of putting them on one side, once you have used them. Cluttered surfaces are the worst enemy of quick cooking. I'm sorry to have to tell you that this also means washing up and putting away – not piling things up or leaving them to drain, so that you spend valuable time hunting the measuring spoon, only to find it lurking under an upturned milk jug.

I don't assume that everyone has elaborate and expensive equipment, so most of the recipes have been tested and timed on the basis of chopping and preparing by hand. One or two actually do need a blender or liquidizer if you are to finish the recipe within the half hour, but in each case this is indicated, so that you don't get half-way through the cooking and then find you have to spend ages trying to sieve the immutable and developing housemaid's elbow in the process. I am not an aficionado of the pressure cooker and have therefore not mentioned it in my recipes, although those of you who have one will know its time- and energy-saving virtues, particularly for casseroles, and may well use it, in addition to my suggestions, for reducing the cooking time of potatoes and other root vegetables.

Of course, if you are the sort of perfectionist who cuts carrots into slices of exactly the same widths, then you are obviously going to need more time than I take. But I was one of those commuters who did a full day's work and then came home to prepare a family meal in the shortest possible time, and my half hour is not taken at the sort of speed that requires spiked running shoes or would qualify me for any Olympic medal. I work at a normal, untrained pace in the belief that while speed is not an excuse for sloppiness, perfectionism in everyday cooking is for the *haute cuisine oiseaux*.

I would simply like you to feel that if you only have half an hour you can pick up this book and produce something tasty and interesting. Or, if you have a spare half hour in an afternoon or evening, you can look ahead and prepare something for the following day.

Quick cookery is basically a question of organization and until you become sufficiently practised, I suggest you try one course at a time. The main courses are nearly all 'instant' – only one or two need an overnight marinade – and several include vegetables in the cooking, so you don't need to do them separately. I have tried to give a wide variety of ideas for starters and puddings, as the easiest way for the quick cook to win a reputation for variety and ingenuity and 'I don't know how you do it in the time' is to concentrate on beginnings and endings planned round a very simply grilled main course, maybe with rice or buttered noodles, which take only about 5 minutes to cook. Several of the soups and puddings are ready to eat immediately, but will also keep overnight, if you are able to plan a day ahead.

Kitchen Planning

A place for everything and everything in its place is a boringly smug piece of advice, but it is a great time-saver. You need to be able to put out your hand in the dark and not land on the curry paste when you wanted mixed herbs, or the Worcestershire sauce when you wanted Tabasco. I have never had an enormous kitchen with masses of cupboards and batteries of this and that, and I have found it a positive advantage to have a small space with everything within easy reach. So I keep pans in one cupboard, bowls and oven-proof plates and dishes in another; spices on one shelf, herbs on another; savoury sauces, sweet flavourings, alcohol, each in an allotted space; baking things together – flour, cornflour, baking powder, dried fruit, nuts; and on another shelf sugars, coffee, gelatine.

Things I Couldn't Do Without

This sub-heading is more precise than you might think. Having shared flats and borrowed houses in various parts of the world, I have been amazed at the lack of what I would consider to be kitchen essentials, and have come to the conclusion that the owners of such kitchens are either basically mean or much more inventive than I. So I would not presume to suggest a basic *batterie de cuisine* – I simply pass on my own preferences.

Chopping board. I use one side for savoury, one side for sweet things. Mine happens to bend in the middle, so I know which side is which, but you could always dab a spot of paint on the sweet side so that you don't confuse them. Garlic-flavoured apple flan is not considered to be a gastronomic delight.

Knives. Every cookbook you have ever read will tell you to buy the best knives you can afford and I am not going to contradict them. Blunt knives slip and cut fingers more readily than sharp ones and anyway, you waste a lot of time hacking at things instead of cutting through them cleanly. Choose the sizes that feel most comfortable for you – my favourites are a 3-inch paring knife, a 4-inch cook's knife, a bread knife and a carving knife.

Kitchen scissors.   Not absolutely essential, but quicker for snipping off rinds and cutting bacon into small strips.

Kitchen shears.   You can buy quite inexpensive ones that will serve as scissors, but are sharp enough to double up as poultry shears, too. Very useful for those times when you thought you had enough time to roast a whole chicken and find, after all, that you need to joint it.

Measuring spoons.   Actually, I only bought these so that I could give exact measurements in these recipes. I normally use ordinary spoons and you can, too, if you are a good guesser. If you haven't had much experience, though, stick to the graded spoons.

Two measuring jugs.   I like pint-size graduated jugs, but a pint jug and a ½-pint one would do. Two are essential, as you will always find one needs to be washed up just as you want it for the next course.

Pans.   I can't bear the ordinary black non-stick sort, but I do find the grey non-stick more durable, easier to clean and less liable to peel after a couple of years. Non-stick pans are particularly valuable for slimmers, as you can use much less fat in them than you would need to prevent food sticking to an ordinary pan.

One 10-inch sauté pan with a lid.   This is absolutely my favourite pan, and is indispensable for speed as it is deep enough to add liquids to, and large enough to spread things out so that they cook evenly and quickly.

One omelette pan.   The size will depend on how many you usually cook for. A 6-inch one is big enough for anyone living alone and is best for making pancakes, too. But I see no objection to making a large omelette and cutting it in half, so if you cook for two or more, opt for an 8-inch size. You aren't going to make omelettes when you are trying to impress guests, so the perfect individual omelette doesn't arise.

Three saucepans.   A 6-inch for melting things – perfect for balancing a 1-pint bowl on top if you are dissolving gelatine or chocolate over hot water. One 8-inch and one 9-inch pan. No point in bothering with small pans. If you aren't going to fiddle about with potatoes you need more vegetable capacity, and if you are cooking pasta for four you need plenty of water to cook it in if you are to avoid a sticky lump.

Deep frier. You only need this if you cook a lot of chips. I never do, as I hate the smell, and there are only two recipes in this book that need deep frying, so if you haven't already got one, don't bother.

One straight-sided 1½-pint soufflé dish.

One deep-sided flat dish for browning under the grill.

Two flat plates, heatproof. Tin will do. One for roasting nuts and for pre-heating when you need a plate to keep things warm on top of the grill. The other I keep next to the chopping board as a debris plate to hold parings and other bits before I throw them away.

Ramekins – useful for starters and afters.

Fast-boil 3-pint electric kettle. Vital.

Colander.

Three mixing bowls. 1-pint, 1½-pint, 3-pint.

Large sieve.

Grater.

Large metal spoon – the size you get in a set of hanging tools.

Baking tray.

Rubber spatula – the plastic ones don't bend enough.

Wire tray for cooling.

Loose-bottomed flan tin, 8-inch.

Four wooden spoons.

Greaseproof paper, kitchen paper and *clingfilm* for wrapping, draining and covering things.

Bean slicer – simple hand-operated one which strings the beans and slices them in one go as you pull them through.

Pastry cutters.

The one piece of expensive equipment I would thoroughly commend to the attention of any speed merchant is the food processor. I used to be mad about the food mixer when I did a lot of baking, but no quick cook has the time to fix and clean all the attachments needed for mincing, dripping oil and so on. The food processor does the whole job with one double blade in one bowl. It

will mince, chop, grind, make pastry and liquidize, all with the one
blade. With two simply-fitted discs it will grate and slice as well.
Wonderful for all those fiddly jobs like making breadcrumbs,
chopping parsley, grating cheese. You can do all these things whenever you have a spare moment and store them in bags in the freezer
or fridge. You can also liquidize soups and purée fruits without the
bother of sieving.

I realize, of course, that such a machine is one of the most expensive small electrical items in the kitchen and for this reason there are
relatively few recipes in this book which depend on a processor for
success. Many people have liquidizers, which can be used with equal
effect to blend or to purée, but even if you have no electrical aids
at all, you can still make most of these recipes – and still in half an
hour. I mention the processor simply because I do think it is the
time-saver of the future – an enormous boon to cooks with a
minimum of time to chop and slice and mince. Most of the major
kitchen equipment companies have brought out their own version
of the processor and the only disadvantage, compared with a mixer,
is that they do not beat air into mixtures quite so successfully – so
sponge cake and meringue are better made with a rotary whisk or
beater. But this problem will no doubt be overcome – some
companies already provide special blades or spherical bowls so that
the cake-making facility is provided, too.

Some of you may hesitate to invest in a processor because you
wonder how much you will use it. I have to admit that I thought of
processors at first as just another toy to make us spend more money,
thinking that I would use it relatively little. In fact, I use it so much I
never put it away, as I did my mixer, which was in service once a
week. My processor is always to hand and in use every day. The one
stipulation I would make is that you should buy one with the
largest capacity you can afford. A food processor is no use at all if it
is too small – reduced by the manufacturers to keep the price down
and 'fill a gap in the market'. If you live alone you don't need one
and if you are cooking regularly for two or more you are better off
with the largest capacity you can find. The extra size is time-saving
for day-to-day cooking – otherwise you are wasting time blending
in batches instead of all at once – and is invaluable when you are
entertaining. Once you have decided to make the initial outlay on

such a machine, which should last many years, the extra cost for a larger model is relatively small.

Store Cupboard

So few people have larders any more that what we are really talking about is a couple of wall cupboards, a fridge and possibly a freezer, or at least a one-star compartment in the fridge. I have therefore tried to keep essential ingredients to a minimum. You will have to buy main ingredients as you go, but if you have the following items always in stock, you have the basis for every recipe in this book:

Dry goods: plain flour, baking powder, granulated sugar, caster sugar, soft brown sugar, digestive and gingernut biscuits (for instant biscuit crusts), sultanas, blanched almonds, roasted hazelnuts, pine kernels, long grain rice (I always use the American easy-cook sort – no time for failure), spaghetti, tagliatelle, noodles, vermicelli, gelatine, corn oil, olive oil, wine vinegar, Tabasco, Worcestershire sauce, soya sauce, tomato paste, chicken and beef stock cubes, salt, black pepper, French and English made mustard, instant coffee, plain chocolate.

Extras or alternatives for low-cholesterol cooking: sunflower oil, polyunsaturated margarine, skimmed dried milk.

Dairy goods: butter, eggs, Cheddar cheese, Parmesan, Edam for slimmers.

Herbs: Dried herbs lose their flavour quickly, so although you can vary your stock according to your preferences, I have kept the suggestions to the ones I feel are most useful, or remain most faithful to the fresh flavour. These are mixed herbs, oregano, dill, bay leaves and tarragon. I would never use dried parsley or dried basil, but if you have space to grow them – they do perfectly well in pots – they are very useful flavours. Thyme is a useful herb, too, and acceptable in dried form, but it is very easy to grow and makes a decorative, as well as flavoursome, plant. Cut parsley, of course, is easily bought from greengrocers, but basil has a very short season and I find it worth growing and freezing in little packets of 1 tablespoon each. I do the same with parsley.

Spices: These have a longer life than herbs, but even so I don't believe in having a complete range unless you are very keen on

Eastern flavourings, most of which, like a real curry, take forever to prepare in order to marry all the flavourings in their correct proportions. So I stick mostly to curry paste (much better than curry powder), coriander, cumin, caraway seeds, cloves, chilli powder, paprika, cayenne, cardamom, garam masala, nutmeg (whole keeps longer than powdered), ground ginger. I don't like garlic salt and prefer to use fresh garlic.

Sweet flavourings: cinnamon, vanilla pod or real vanilla essence (McCormicks is the only one I would buy as all the rest taste synthetic), liquid sweetener for slimmers.

Alcohol: sherry, whit evermouth, Marsala, brandy, rum, port (only if you drink it normally, as only two recipes use it), red and white wine. Some cooks will tell you that you can't use cheap wine and still achieve first-class results. That's fine for coq au vin, but it doesn't apply when you are adding a couple of tablespoons to a sauce, so keep wine in the fridge that is not so expensive that it will break your heart to pour it into the pan, nor so mouth-puckering that you can't cheer yourself up with a little glass if you feel like it. Tia Maria, Grand Marnier, Crème de Menthe – all in miniatures if they are not something you normally drink.

Freezer: shortcrust pastry (bought, or your own, if you have enough freezer space), puff pastry, raspberries, blackberries, blackcurrants, apple slices (saves a lot of peeling), concentrated orange and grapefruit juice, plus four useful stand-by vegetables – chosen because the fresh versions take so long to prepare – green beans, peas, sweet corn and leaf spinach.

Cans: To my taste there are very few goods worth stocking in cans. Anchovies are useful, and pineapple is good for sweet-and-sour dishes. Pulse beans – kidney beans, butter beans and cannellini beans – are handy for those interested in the low-cholesterol chapter, and this is only in the interests of speed, not texture.

Quick Tips

Buy parsley, or cut your own, in large batches whenever you have a spare 10 minutes. Chop it and place tablespoons of it on squares of clingfilm. Fold into little parcels and keep in a tub in the freezer. Just add to recipes as required.

Make up similar bags of white breadcrumbs in, say, 2-oz batches.

Grate ends of cheese and freeze in 1-oz packs.

Keep a bottle of pure lemon juice in the fridge to use in recipes which do not also require lemon rind. Saves squeezing.

When cooking pastry dishes, always place a baking tray in the oven when you pre-heat and stand made-up dishes on it. This will conduct the heat and will cook the base of the pie or flan more quickly.

Keep a flour sifter full of seasoned flour for sprinkling. Try a proportion of 4 oz flour to 4 level teaspoons salt and 2 level teaspoons ground black pepper.

Several recipes use fresh, skinned tomatoes. Get into the habit of boiling a kettleful of water as you start cooking. Place the tomatoes in a bowl, pour boiling water over, leave for 1 minute. This will soften the skins and make them easy to peel. You can do the same thing with peaches.

Talking of tomatoes, it is totally unnecessary to de-seed them when you chop. Some cooks will tell you to do so, but I am convinced it is all a professional conspiracy to make the rest of us feel inadequate. We should not be frightened by our own kitchens – cooking is a creative activity and should be fun. When you have learned to be a quick cook, time is always on your side.

NOTE: *Do not compare imperial and metric measurements – use one or the other. The best measure for the recipe has been given in each case, and where equivalents appear inconsistent, this may be because the ingredient is usually sold in the pack size given.*

SOUPS AND STARTERS

You can open a can of soup and slosh in a tablespoon of sherry and call that quick cooking if you like, but you aren't going to fool anybody who knows about food. And there really isn't any need to, particularly if you have a liquidizer or processor. The basis of all good home-made soups is a well-flavoured stock, and I can't understand why the stock-pot habit has died out. It isn't necessary to keep a huge pot simmering away at an unhygienic temperature for days and weeks. I never buy frozen chickens, but always fresh ones with giblets. These I cover with water and simmer with an onion for half an hour. I keep the liver separate and freeze each one until I have enough to make a pilaf. Why buy chicken livers when they come with the giblets, anyway? Or, when the chicken is eaten, I put the carcase in a large pan with an onion – and a carrot and a piece of celery if I happen to have them around – cover with water and simmer, covered, for a couple of hours – it will accommodate a favourite television programme happily. When cool, the bones and vegetables are removed and the liquid put in the fridge overnight so that any fat solidifies. When skimmed, this makes an excellent basis for soup. Vegetables can be simmered in it with seasoning (don't season it when boiling the bones, otherwise you can end up with oversalted soup, as often happens when you use stock cubes), and then you simply purée them or rub them through a sieve. There's no need to take extra tedious time thickening them with flour or cornflour, as the purée makes its own thickening. You can do the same thing with beef bones, but I find lamb has too fatty a flavour. For fish stock see page 26.

As for other starters, simple patés do need a little pre-planning, because they are better left to chill for a couple of hours, but the actual making time is minimal. And don't neglect vegetables as a starter – in the right combinations of colour and texture and with interesting dressing they can be nutritious, delicious and not too filling.

Avocado Soup
TIME 30 minutes   SERVES 6

Best made in a blender and with really ripe avocados. Even the over-ripe ones, which are usually cheaper, will do for this recipe.

2 large ripe avocados	*2 large ripe avocados*
1 pint cold chicken stock or	*600 ml cold chicken stock or*
1½ chicken stock cubes	* 1½ chicken stock cubes*
5 fl oz single cream	*150 ml single cream*
salt and black pepper	*salt and black pepper*
1 dessertspoon lemon juice	*1 dessertspoon lemon juice*
½ teaspoon Tabasco	*½ teaspoon Tabasco*
2 tablespoons chopped chives	*2 tablespoons chopped chives*

If using stock cubes, put a cupful of water on to boil. Skin the avocados, remove the stones, and place the flesh in a blender or processor. Dissolve the stock cubes in a little boiling water and make up to 1 pint (600 ml) with cold water. Or use cold stock. Gradually add to the blender or processor and blend until smooth. Add cream, salt and pepper to taste, lemon juice and Tabasco and blend again. This will take about 10 minutes.

Pour into a bowl or tureen and chill for time remaining, or until required. Sprinkle with chives just before serving.

Cauliflower Soup
TIME 30 minutes   SERVES 6   [F]

You need a blender or processor for this to get a smooth texture.

1¾ pints chicken stock or 2 chicken stock cubes	*1 litre chicken stock or 2 chicken stock cubes*
salt and black pepper	*salt and black pepper*
1 cauliflower	*1 cauliflower*
1 tablespoon chopped parsley	*1 tablespoon chopped parsley*
5 fl oz single cream	*150 ml single cream*
paprika	*paprika*

Place the stock, or the equivalent amount of water plus the stock cubes, in a saucepan and bring to the boil with salt to taste. Meanwhile, remove the tough stems of the cauliflower, break off the florets and add them, with any of the more tender bits of green, to the stock. Cover and simmer gently for 15 minutes or until the cauliflower is just tender. Meanwhile chop the parsley.

Ladle the soup into a blender or processor and blend until smooth. Return to the pan, stir in the parsley and cream, and adjust the seasoning. Heat through without boiling, pour into soup cups and sprinkle with paprika.

Curried Tomato Soup
TIME 30 minutes   SERVES 4   [F]

If rubbed through a sieve, this recipe makes 1¼ pints of thinnish soup. The texture is thicker and the quantity about 1½ pints if a blender or processor is used. You can of course blend your own curry spices if you prefer.

12 fl oz chicken stock or 1 chicken stock cube	*350 ml chicken stock or 1 chicken stock cube*
1 oz butter	*30 g butter*
6 oz onion	*175 g onion*

1 clove garlic	*1 clove garlic*
1 lb ripe tomatoes	*500 g ripe tomatoes*
1 dessertspoon curry powder	*1 dessertspoon curry powder*
salt and black pepper	*salt and black pepper*
5 fl oz soured cream	*150 ml soured cream*

Heat the chicken stock in a small pan. In a kettle, boil enough water to cover the tomatoes, plus another 12 fl oz (350 ml) if using a stock cube. Heat the butter slowly in a large saucepan. Chop the onion and fry gently for 3 minutes. Meanwhile cover the tomatoes with boiling water, skin and chop roughly. Add the curry powder to the pan and stir over a medium heat for 2 minutes. Crush the garlic with a little salt and add to the pan with the tomatoes. Add the stock, or the stock cube dissolved in 12 fl oz (350 ml) water. Bring to the boil, cover and simmer for 10 minutes.

Rub the vegetables through a sieve or use a blender or processor. Return to the pan, adjust the seasoning, heat through and stir in the soured cream just before serving.

This soup can also be served cold, in which case keep the cream until the soup is chilled and swirl a spoonful into each individual soup cup.

Gazpacho
TIME 30 minutes   SERVES 4   [F]

There are plenty of fancy recipes for gazpacho which include green peppers and cucumber and all sorts. But this simple version was given to me by an award-winning cook in Spain and was always served at his table without any embellishments. You need a blender or processor to make it for 4 people and still allow time to chill. Otherwise, if you are rubbing through a sieve, it will take you 30 minutes to make half the quantity for 2 people. Chilling time will be extra, but you can always do that overnight.

1 large clove garlic	*1 large clove garlic*
salt	*salt*
2 oz fresh white breadcrumbs	*60 g fresh white breadcrumbs*
2 lbs really ripe tomatoes	*900 g really ripe tomatoes*

1 teaspoon wine vinegar
3 tablespoons olive oil

1 teaspoon wine vinegar
3 tablespoons olive oil

Boil enough water to cover the tomatoes – about 2 pints (1.25 litres). Meanwhile crush the garlic with a little salt and grate the breadcrumbs. Pour boiling water over the tomatoes to loosen the skins. Remove the skins, chop the tomatoes roughly and place in a blender or processor. Add the garlic and breadcrumbs and blend until smooth. Add the vinegar and dribble in the oil gradually, blending all the time. I don't mind a few pips, but if you do, pour the mixture through a sieve. Adjust the seasoning to taste, pour into a bowl and chill for 15 minutes.

If sieving by hand, place the breadcrumbs in a bowl and rub the tomatoes through the sieve onto the crumbs. Then re-sieve the mixture before blending in the garlic, vinegar and oil.

Leek and Potato Soup

TIME 30 minutes   SERVES 4   [F]

This soup can be served hot, but doesn't get the grand name of Vichyssoise until it is chilled. Leeks are not easy to sieve, so you really need a blender.

1 pint chicken stock or
   1 chicken stock cube
6 oz potatoes
salt
8 oz leeks
3 fl oz single cream
1 tablespoon chopped chives

600 ml chicken stock or
   1 chicken stock cube
175 g potatoes
salt
250 g leeks
80 ml single cream
1 tablespoon chopped chives

Place the stock, or stock cube plus 1 pint (600 ml) water, in a saucepan and bring to the boil. Meanwhile, peel the potatoes and cut into small dice. Add to the pan with a pinch of salt. Trim the leeks, slit vertically and run under the cold tap to remove dirt and grit. Chop finely and add to the pan. Cover and simmer for 15–20 minutes or until the vegetables are just tender. Pour into a blender or pro-

cessor and blend until smooth. Stir in the cream, adjust the seasoning
and serve hot or chill overnight. Sprinkle with chives just before
serving.

Hot Lemon Soup
TIME 30 minutes   SERVES 4

This is my version of the Greek soup avgolemono. You can adjust
the amount of lemon to your own taste, but you should use home-
made chicken stock (see page 1) and not cubes for the best results.

2 pints chicken stock	*1·25 litres chicken stock*
salt and black pepper	*salt and black pepper*
2 oz long grain rice	*60 g long grain rice*
3 eggs	*3 eggs*
2 lemons	*2 lemons*
1 tablespoon chopped parsley	*1 tablespoon chopped parsley*

Place the stock in a saucepan and heat to boiling point. Add the rice
and a good pinch of salt and simmer, uncovered, for 15 minutes, or
until the rice is soft. Place the eggs in a bowl and whisk. Squeeze the
lemon juice and beat into the eggs. Add a ladle of hot stock, beat,
then add another ladle of stock and beat again.

Remove the pan of stock from the heat and gradually pour in the
egg mixture. Season with pepper and more salt if necessary. Return
the soup to a low heat and whisk until it thickens slightly – don't
boil, or it will curdle. Pour into soup cups and sprinkle with parsley.

Lettuce Soup
TIME 30 minutes   SERVES 6   [F]

This is an excellent way of using the tough, outside leaves of lettuce.
It can be sieved – takes about 5 minutes to rub through – but is
easier with a blender or processor.

1¾ pints chicken stock or
  2 chicken stock cubes
1 oz butter
1 medium onion (4 oz)
8 oz potatoes
outside leaves of a large
  lettuce (keeping just the heart
  for salad)
salt and black pepper
4 tablespoons single cream
  (optional)

1 litre chicken stock or
  2 chicken stock cubes
30 g butter
1 medium onion (125 g)
250 g potatoes
outside leaves of a large
  lettuce (keeping just the heart
  for salad)
salt and black pepper
4 tablespoons single cream
  (optional)

Boil 1¾ pints (1 litre) water in a kettle or heat the stock in a saucepan. Meanwhile, melt the butter in a large saucepan and chop the onion. Fry without browning for 3 minutes. Peel and dice the potatoes and add to the pan. Cook for a further 2 minutes while washing and shredding the lettuce. Either dissolve the stock cubes in the boiling water and add to the pan, or use the hot stock. Add to the pan with the lettuce, cover and simmer gently for 15 minutes.

Rub the vegetables through a sieve or purée in a blender or processor, and season to taste. Return to the pan, bring to boiling point and remove from the heat before stirring in the cream. Otherwise, chill until required, pour into individual dishes and swirl the cream on top of each.

Sorrel Soup

TIME 30 minutes   SERVES 4

As I love fresh herbs, but am not a great gardener, my flavourings depend on the survival of the fittest and sorrel withstands all sorts of neglect and foul weather. It has a sharp flavour, so you may have to experiment with the quantities to get it right for your taste.

1½ pints chicken stock or
  2 chicken stock cubes
1 oz butter
1 small onion (2 oz)

900 ml chicken stock or
  2 chicken stock cubes
30 g butter
1 small onion (60 g)

8 oz fresh sorrel leaves	*250 g fresh sorrel leaves*
salt and black pepper	*salt and black pepper*
5 fl oz single cream	*150 ml single cream*

Heat the stock in a pan or boil 1½ pints (900 ml) water in a kettle. Heat the butter in a saucepan. Chop the onion finely and add, cooking gently for 3 minutes without browning. Meanwhile strip the sorrel leaves from the stalks, wash, shake dry and add to the pan. Stir in the stock with a pinch of salt, or dissolve the stock cube in the boiling water and add. Simmer for 5 minutes, then put through a blender or processor. Return to the pan and stir in the cream. Adjust the seasoning and re-heat gently without boiling.

Cheese Soup with Croûtons
TIME 30 minutes · SERVES 4

Gouda cheese is suggested for this soup as it melts easily, but I have made it successfully with Edam, which is lower in calories.

15 fl oz chicken stock or
  1 chicken stock cube
	450 ml chicken stock or
	  1 chicken stock cube

1½ oz butter	*40 g butter*
1½ oz flour	*40 g flour*
1 pint milk	*600 ml milk*
4 oz frozen peas	*125 g frozen peas*
6 oz Gouda cheese	*175 g Gouda cheese*
2 tablespoons chopped parsley	*2 tablespoons chopped parsley*
salt and black pepper	*salt and black pepper*
1 tablespoon corn oil	*1 tablespoon corn oil*

2 slices, ¼ inch thick, from a
  large white loaf
	2 slices, 1 cm thick, from a
	  large white loaf

Place the chicken stock in a pan and heat to simmering point, or boil 15 fl oz (450 ml) water in a kettle. Melt the butter in a saucepan, sprinkle in the flour and stir over a gentle heat for 1 minute. Gradually add the milk and cook, stirring, for 3 minutes, until thickened and smooth.

Dissolve the stock cube in the boiling water and stir in, or add the heated stock. Add the peas and simmer for 5 minutes.

Meanwhile, grate the cheese and chop the parsley. Remove the pan from the heat, add the cheese and stir until completely melted. Return to a very low heat – do not re-boil – and stir in the parsley. Add salt and pepper to taste.

Heat the oil in a frying pan, remove the crusts from the bread, cut into $\frac{1}{4}$-inch cubes and fry until golden on all sides. Pour the soup into individual cups and sprinkle with the croûtons.

Cream Cheese and Olive Tartlets

TIME 30 minutes   MAKES 8 tartlets

If you have a food processor, the time for this recipe can be reduced by blending the pastry ingredients instead of rubbing by hand.

4 oz plain flour	*120 g plain flour*
1 oz lard	*30 g lard*
1 oz butter	*30 g butter*
salt and black pepper	*salt and black pepper*
1 egg	*1 egg*
6 oz cream cheese	*175 g cream cheese*
1 oz pimento-stuffed olives	*30 g pimento-stuffed olives*
1 oz Cheddar cheese	*30 g Cheddar cheese*

Heat the oven to Gas 6; 400° F; 200° C.

Rub the flour, fats and a small pinch of salt together. Add 1$\frac{1}{2}$ tablespoons of cold water and mix to a pliable dough. Roll out thinly on a floured surface and cut out 8 rounds with a 3-inch (8-cm) cutter. Grease 8 patty tins and line with the pastry.

Beat the egg and add gradually to the cream cheese, beating until smooth and thick. Do not make too runny. Chop the olives and stir in with salt and black pepper to taste. Divide the mixture between the pastry cases. Grate the Cheddar cheese, sprinkle over the tartlets, and bake at the top of the oven for 15 minutes, until risen and golden. Serve hot.

Cheese and Olive Puffs

TIME 30 minutes   MAKES 16

4 oz Cheddar cheese	120 g Cheddar cheese
2 eggs	2 eggs
1 tablespoon pale ale or soda water	1 tablespoon pale ale or soda water
¼ teaspoon salt	¼ teaspoon salt
pepper	pepper
2 tablespoons plain flour	2 tablespoons plain flour
½ teaspoon baking powder	½ teaspoon baking powder
16 pimento-stuffed olives	16 pimento-stuffed olives
deep corn oil for frying	deep corn oil for frying

Grate the cheese into a bowl. Separate the eggs and beat the yolks into the cheese with the ale or soda water, salt and pepper to taste. Sift the flour and baking powder onto the mixture and stir in. Whisk the egg whites stiffly and fold in gently until well blended. Place in the fridge for 10 minutes.

Drain the olives. Put the corn oil on a medium heat. Place 16 teaspoons of the mixture on a well floured board and press an olive in the centre of each, covering completely with the cheese dough. Fry in the deep oil for 3–4 minutes until golden and puffed up, and serve on a bed of lettuce as a starter or with drinks as a party snack.

Cucumber and Prawn Dip

TIME 30 minutes   SERVES 4

This is a flossy version of the Greek cucumber and yogurt dip. If serving it for a party, it looks pretty piled into scallop shells.

1 cucumber	1 cucumber
salt	salt
1 clove garlic	1 clove garlic
2 tablespoons chopped fresh mint	2 tablespoons chopped fresh mint
16 fl oz natural yogurt	½ litre natural yogurt

| 4 pieces pitta bread | *4 pieces pitta bread* |
| 6 oz shelled prawns | *175 g shelled prawns* |

Cut the cucumber in half. Peel one half, cut into $\frac{1}{4}$-inch (1-cm) dice, and place in a colander. Sprinkle with salt and leave to drain. Grate the other cucumber half, including the skin, into a sieve and squeeze out the excess moisture by hand. Crush the garlic with a little salt and place in a bowl with the mint, yogurt and grated cucumber. This takes about 10 minutes. Chill the mixture for 15 minutes.

Just before needed, heat the pitta under the grill. Turn the cucumber dice onto kitchen paper, pat dry and stir into the yogurt with the prawns. Turn into individual dishes and serve with the hot pitta.

Aubergine Dip
TIME 30 minutes plus chilling   SERVES 4   [F]

The original Turkish name for this dish means aubergine salad, but this is misleading and as it makes a good dip for drinks parties, as well as a tasty hors d'oeuvre, I have renamed it. You really do need a blender or processor. Aubergine behaves like old rags when you try to sieve it.

2 aubergines (about $1\frac{1}{2}$ lbs)	*2 aubergines (about 750 g)*
1 or 2 cloves garlic	*1 or 2 cloves garlic*
2 tablespoons lemon juice	*2 tablespoons lemon juice*
4 tablespoons olive oil	*4 tablespoons olive oil*
1 dessertspoon chopped parsley	*1 dessertspoon chopped parsley*
salt and black pepper	*salt and black pepper*

Heat the grill and toast the aubergines until the skins are black and blistering, turning to cook all sides. This will take about 15 minutes. Place them on a chopping board, split them, and spoon the flesh into a large sieve. Press with a spoon (or a flat potato masher is a good implement for this) to extract as much juice as possible, otherwise the taste may be bitter. Place the flesh in a blender or processor. Crush the garlic with a little salt and squeeze the lemon juice. Add both to the blender or processor. Gradually add the oil, blending all the time until the mixture is light. Chop the parsley and add with salt and pepper to taste. Pile in a bowl and chill well. Serve with hot pitta, as in previous recipe.

Avocado Dip

TIME 30 minutes   SERVES 4

½ a small green pepper	*½ a small green pepper*
2 tablespoons chopped onion	*2 tablespoons chopped onion*
1 clove garlic	*1 clove garlic*
salt	*salt*
1 teaspoon chilli powder	*1 teaspoon chilli powder*
2 ripe avocados	*2 ripe avocados*
1–2 tablespoons lemon juice	*1–2 tablespoons lemon juice*
lettuce	*lettuce*
4 firm tomatoes	*4 firm tomatoes*

De-seed and chop the pepper and chop the onion. Crush the garlic with a little salt. Mix together and add the chilli powder. Halve and stone the avocados and place the flesh in a bowl with the lemon juice. Mash with a fork until smooth. Fold in the pepper and onion mixture and adjust the seasoning to taste. Chill for 15 minutes.

Arrange the lettuce on individual plates, spoon the avocado mixture in the centre and decorate with quartered tomatoes.

Avocado Mousse

TIME 30 minutes plus setting   SERVES 6

Serve this mousse straight from the dish you make it in. If you turn it out of a mould and it has to stand for long, it may go brown. It can be sieved or made in a blender or processor.

½ oz gelatine	*15 g gelatine*
¼ pint whipping cream	*150 ml whipping cream*

3 rounded tablespoons mayonnaise	*3 rounded tablespoons mayonnaise*
2 large ripe avocados	*2 large ripe avocados*
1 teaspoon grated onion	*1 teaspoon grated onion*
salt and pepper	*salt and pepper*
1 teaspoon Worcestershire sauce	*1 teaspoon Worcestershire sauce*
2 tomatoes	*2 tomatoes*

Place ¼ pint (150 ml) cold water in a small bowl and sprinkle with the gelatine. Set the bowl over a pan containing a little water and bring to simmering point. Heat until the gelatine dissolves, stirring occasionally. Pour into another bowl (this speeds up the cooling) and add a further ¼ pint (150 ml) of cold water.

Whip the cream and whisk in the mayonnaise. Peel and stone the avocados. Mash the flesh and then rub it through a sieve, or use a blender or processor. Grate the onion into the mixture and fold in the cream with ½ teaspoon of salt and Worcestershire sauce to taste. Lightly stir in the gelatine liquid, adjust the seasoning and pour into a glass dish. Chill overnight. Decorate with quartered tomatoes before serving.

Baked Avocados with Crab

TIME 30 minutes   SERVES 4

Hot avocados make an interesting starter for cooler weather, and as both this version and the following one are fairly rich you need nothing more than a simple grill as a main course. Don't make the mistake of thinking that cooking an avocado will make it tender – you need to start with them ripe.

1 oz butter	*30 g butter*
1 tablespoon chopped onion	*1 tablespoon chopped onion*
3–4 oz crabmeat, fresh or canned	*100–125 g crabmeat, fresh or canned*
2 tablespoons fresh white breadcrumbs	*2 tablespoons fresh white breadcrumbs*

1–2 tablespoons single cream	1–2 tablespoons single cream
salt and pepper	salt and pepper
paprika	paprika
2 ripe avocados	2 ripe avocados
1 oz Cheddar cheese	30 g Cheddar cheese

Heat the oven to Gas 6; 400° F; 200° C.

Melt the butter in a frying pan. Chop the onion finely and cook gently in the butter for 3 minutes without browning. Add the crabmeat and heat through while preparing the breadcrumbs. Stir the crumbs into the crab mixture with the cream, and season with salt, pepper and paprika to taste. Halve the avocados, remove the stones and place them, cavity up, on a shallow ovenproof dish. Spoon the crab mixture into the cavities, grate the cheese on top and bake towards the top of the oven for 20 minutes.

Avocado with Ham and Cheese

TIME 25 minutes   SERVES 4

1 oz butter	25 g butter
1 oz flour	25 g flour
8 fl oz milk	¼ litre milk
3 oz Cheddar cheese	90 g Cheddar cheese
1 oz cooked ham	25 g cooked ham
salt and pepper	salt and pepper
lemon juice	lemon juice
2 ripe avocados	2 ripe avocados

Heat the oven to Gas 6; 400° F; 200° C.

Melt the butter in a small saucepan and sprinkle in the flour. Stir over a gentle heat for 1 minute. Gradually add the milk, stirring until smooth. The mixture should be fairly thick. Remove from the heat and grate the cheese. Stir 1 oz (30 g) of cheese into the sauce. Dice the ham and stir in. Season to taste with salt, pepper and a squeeze of lemon juice.

Halve the avocados, remove the stones, and place them, cavity up, on an ovenproof dish. Spoon the cheese mixture into the cavities, sprinkle with the remaining cheese and bake for 10 minutes, towards the top of the oven. Meanwhile, heat the grill and brown the tops just before serving.

Mushrooms with Garlic Butter
TIME 30 minutes   SERVES 4

I doubt if many people would seriously consider eating rubber-textured snails if it were not for the delicious garlicky butter that goes with them. Serve the same butter with mushrooms and you have a best-of-both worlds starter.

4 oz butter	*125 g butter*
2 tablespoons chopped onion	*2 tablespoons chopped onion*
2 large cloves garlic	*2 large cloves garlic*
2 tablespoons chopped parsley	*2 tablespoons chopped parsley*
salt and black pepper	*salt and black pepper*
24 button mushrooms, each	*24 button mushrooms, each*
not less than 1 inch diameter	* not less than 2 cm diameter*

Heat the oven to Gas 5; 375° F; 190° C.

Melt the butter gently in a small saucepan. Meanwhile, chop the onion finely, crush the garlic with a little salt and chop the parsley. Stir all these into the butter and season to taste.

Wipe the mushrooms and remove the stalks. Dip each mushroom into the butter and arrange on an ovenproof dish just big enough to hold them all, side by side. Pour the flavoured butter over, making sure the centre cavities are filled. Bake for 15 minutes and serve with crusty French bread.

Stuffed Mushrooms
TIME 30 minutes   SERVES 4   [F]

You need ready-prepared breadcrumbs and parsley to do this in the time.

2 oz butter	60 g butter
12 mushrooms, about 2 inch diameter	12 mushrooms, about 5 cm diameter
1 medium onion	1 medium onion
1 clove garlic (optional)	1 clove garlic (optional)
salt and pepper	salt and pepper
2 tablespoons chopped parsley	2 tablespoons chopped parsley
1 oz breadcrumbs	30 g breadcrumbs
1 oz grated Cheddar cheese	30 g grated Cheddar cheese
1 tablespoon grated Parmesan	1 tablespoon grated Parmesan
1 tablespoon chicken stock or milk	1 tablespoon chicken stock or milk

Heat the oven to Gas 6; 400° F; 200° C.

Melt 1 oz (30 g) butter in a small pan. Meanwhile wipe the mushrooms and remove the stalks. Dip the caps in butter and arrange on a shallow ovenproof dish. Heat the remaining butter in a frying pan, chop the onion and cook gently for 3 minutes while chopping the mushroom stalks and crushing the garlic, if used, with a little salt. Add these with the parsley, and cook for 2 more minutes.

Place the breadcrumbs in a bowl, grate the Cheddar cheese and add with the Parmesan. Add the onion mixture and the chicken stock or milk. Season to taste and mix well. Place a teaspoon of the mixture in each mushroom cap and bake at the top of the oven for 15 minutes.

Chinese Greens
TIME 20 minutes   SERVES 4

In Chinese restaurants you may have enjoyed a starter known as
'seaweed'. It was the Chinese food specialist Kenneth Lo who told
me that you can achieve the same result with spring greens. It is
important to wipe the leaves rather than wash them or, if they are
very dirty, to wash and dry them well in advance of cooking. If
they are damp the oil will splash all over the place. It was also
Kenneth Lo who told me that he had been eating monosodium
glutamate in small quantities – no more than a pinch at a time –
most of his adult life, and as he is still a tennis champion at 67 it
doesn't seem to have done him much harm, although, of course, it
is not recommended regularly or in large quantities.

1½ lbs spring greens	*750 g spring greens*
deep corn oil for frying	*deep corn oil for frying*
1 teaspoon sugar	*1 teaspoon sugar*
Knorr Aromat seasoning, or	*Knorr Aromat seasoning or*
monosodium glutamate	*monosodium glutamate*

Remove the hard centre stalk from each leaf, wiping each one with
damp kitchen paper. Place a deep pan of oil on a medium heat.
Shred the greens as finely as you can – no more than ⅛-inch thick.
(The easiest way to do this is to roll up several leaves together and
slice finely across them.) When you have sliced them all the oil will
be hot enough – do not overheat, otherwise the greens will burn.
Place a quarter of the quantity in the pan and cover immediately
with a lid to prevent splashing. After a few seconds you can add
another quarter, covering as before. Then remove the lid and fry
for about 3 minutes.

  Meanwhile, warm a dish. Remove the greens in their basket and
turn onto kitchen paper to drain off any excess oil, then turn into the
warm dish while you cook the remaining greens as before. When
all are cooked and drained, sprinkle with the sugar and Aromat and
serve immediately. Even if the greens are slightly limp when they
first come out of the pan, they crisp up after a minute in the dish.

Spinach with Pine Kernels
TIME 15 minutes   SERVES 4

This is served as a cold hors d'oeuvre in Ibiza. It is made with very
small strips of sobrasado sausage, but if you don't like this, or find it
difficult to get, bacon is an acceptable substitute.

1 lb frozen leaf spinach	*500 g frozen leaf spinach*
2 rashers smoked back bacon	*2 rashers smoked back bacon*
1 oz butter	*30 g butter*
1 medium onion (4 oz)	*1 medium onion (125 g)*
1 oz pine kernels	*25 g pine kernels*
1 clove garlic	*1 clove garlic*
lemon juice	*lemon juice*
salt and black pepper	*salt and black pepper*

Place the spinach in a saucepan with 1 tablespoon of water and heat
gently. Meanwhile, de-rind the bacon and cut into very small
strips. Heat the butter in a sauté pan and fry the bacon over a
medium heat until crisp. Meanwhile chop the onion finely, add to
the bacon and continue to fry gently for 2 or 3 minutes.

Place the pine kernels on a heatproof plate and brown under the
grill. Turn the spinach into a sieve, press out as much water as
possible, and add to the sauté pan. Crush the garlic with a little salt
and add to the spinach. Stir together, separating the spinach leaves
and mixing well with the bacon and onion. Add the pine kernels, a
squeeze of lemon juice and salt and black pepper to taste, and serve
hot or cold.

Pears with Blue Cheese
TIME 10 minutes   SERVES 4

I first tried this starter in France, where the blue cheese used was
Roquefort, which is very extravagant. This version is quite mild
and uses the creamy textured Dolce Latte. You can use Stilton or
any blue cheese and mix it in the proportions you like best.

2 oz cream cheese	60 g cream cheese
2 oz Dolce Latte	60 g Dolce Latte
2 teaspoons mayonnaise	2 teaspoons mayonnaise
salt and black pepper	salt and black pepper
1 lemon	1 lemon
2 large ripe pears	2 large ripe pears
paprika	paprika
curly endive or lettuce	curly endive or lettuce

Place the cream cheese in a bowl and mash with a fork. Add the Dolce Latte and mix well, beating until smooth. Add the mayonnaise and beat again. Season to taste with a very little salt if necessary (the cheese is fairly salty) and black pepper.

Squeeze the lemon juice into a small bowl. Halve and peel the pears and remove the cores. Dip each half into the lemon juice to prevent browning. Fill the cavities with the cheese mixture, and sprinkle with paprika.

Wash the endive or lettuce, arrange on 4 small plates and place a pear half in the centre of each. Serve immediately, or chill for 15 minutes if wished.

Egg and Prawn Ramekins
TIME 25 minutes   SERVES 4

2 eggs	2 eggs
1 oz butter	30 g butter
1 oz flour	30 g flour
½ pint milk	300 ml milk
3 oz grated Cheddar cheese	90 g grated Cheddar cheese
4 oz peeled prawns	125 g peeled prawns
1 tablespoon chopped parsley	1 tablespoon chopped parsley
salt and pepper	salt and pepper

Hard-boil the eggs. Meanwhile, melt the butter in a small saucepan, sprinkle in the flour and stir over a gentle heat for 1 minute. Gradually add the milk, stirring for 2–3 minutes until smooth. Heat the grill. Remove the sauce from the heat, add 2 oz (60 g) of cheese and the prawns. Shell and chop the eggs and add to the mixture. Chop the parsley and add with salt and pepper to taste, and spoon into 4 small ramekins. Sprinkle with the remaining cheese and place under a hot grill for about 3 minutes until golden and bubbling.

Marinaded Kipper Fillets
TIME 10 minutes plus marinade   SERVES 4

12 oz boneless kipper fillets	*350 g boneless kipper fillets*
black pepper	*black pepper*
1 medium Spanish onion (4 oz)	*1 medium Spanish onion (125 g)*
2 tablespoons wine vinegar	*2 tablespoons wine vinegar*
1 tablespoon lemon juice	*1 tablespoon lemon juice*
9 tablespoons corn oil	*9 tablespoons corn oil*

Remove any skin from the kipper fillets and slice thinly into strips, like smoked salmon. Lay the strips in a shallow dish and sprinkle with black pepper. Slice the onion and place on top. Place the vinegar and lemon juice in a small bowl and whisk in the oil with a fork. Pour over the fish and leave to marinade overnight. Serve with wholemeal bread and butter.

Herrings in Soured Cream
TIME 30 minutes   SERVES 4

This dish is best made with Matjes herring, but if you are feeling economical pickled herrings will do.

12 oz Matjes herring	*350 g Matjes herring*
1 small onion (2 oz)	*1 small onion (60 g)*
2 small gherkins	*2 small gherkins*
2 Granny Smith apples	*2 Granny Smith apples*
1 teaspoon lemon juice	*1 teaspoon lemon juice*
1 tablespoon sugar	*1 tablespoon sugar*

5 fl oz soured cream	*150 ml soured cream*
lettuce	*lettuce*
black olives	*black olives*

Cut the herrings into thin strips and place in a bowl. Slice the onion thinly, dice the gherkins, and peel and chop the apples. Add all these to the bowl with the lemon juice, and toss together.

Stir the sugar into the soured cream and fold into the mixture. Chill for 15 minutes, pile onto a bed of lettuce and decorate with black olives.

Kipper Pâté
TIME 30 minutes   SERVES 4   [F]

Smoked fish pâtés are always popular and you can vary these basic recipes for kipper pâté and smoked mackerel pâté (next recipe) with whichever smoked fish you fancy. It can be pounded or mashed if you like a rough texture. Otherwise, for smooth creamy pâtés, you need a blender or processor.

7 oz boneless kipper fillets	*200 g boneless kipper fillets*
1 lemon	*1 lemon*
4 oz butter	*120 g butter*
1 small onion (about 2 oz)	*1 small onion (about 60 g)*
1 dessertspoon chopped parsley	*1 dessertspoon chopped parsley*
1 tablespoon double cream	*1 tablespoon double cream*
salt and black pepper	*salt and black pepper*

Remove any skin from the kipper fillets and place in a pan with a little water. Simmer gently for 10 minutes, or until the fish will flake easily. You can use frozen fillets and cook in the bag. Meanwhile, squeeze the lemon, soften the butter, grate the onion and chop the parsley.

Drain the fish, flake it into a bowl and cool for 5 minutes. Add the lemon juice and mash together. Gradually add the softened butter and beat well. Stir in the onion, parsley and cream, with salt and pepper to taste. Chill until required – overnight if you wish.

Smoked Mackerel Pâté
TIME 15 minutes plus chilling   SERVES 4   [F]

8 oz smoked mackerel fillet	*250 g smoked mackerel fillet*
3 tablespoons lemon juice	*3 tablespoons lemon juice*
4 oz cream cheese	*125 g cream cheese*
2 tablespoons single cream	*2 tablespoons single cream*
4 oz cottage cheese	*125 g cottage cheese*
salt and black pepper	*salt and black pepper*
paprika	*paprika*

Remove the skin and any bones from the mackerel fillet and place the flesh in a bowl. Add the lemon juice and mash well until smooth. In another bowl, mash the cream cheese with the cream until soft. Sieve the cottage cheese on top and beat well. Fold in the fish and add more lemon juice, if necessary, with salt and pepper to taste.

If you have a blender or processor, simply blend all the ingredients until smooth. Pile into a terrine and chill for 2 hours or overnight. Sprinkle with paprika and serve with hot toast.

Taramasalata
TIME 25 minutes   SERVES 4   [F]

You can, of course, buy ready-made taramasalata, but the quality varies enormously. Quite the worst I ever tasted was the colour of raspberry blancmange. It should be very pale, peachy pink, and if it is at all rosy you know it contains artificial colouring. You can make it by hand, or in a blender or processor.

4 oz smoked cod's roe	*125 g smoked cod's roe*
4–6 oz white bread, crusts removed	*125–175 g white bread, crusts removed*
1 tablespoon grated onion	*1 tablespoon grated onion*
1 clove garlic	*1 clove garlic*
1 large lemon giving 2 tablespoons juice	*1 large lemon giving 2 tablespoons juice*

6–8 tablespoons olive oil
1 tablespoon milk

6–8 tablespoons olive oil
1 tablespoon milk

If making by hand, remove the skin from the roe and place the fish in a bowl or mortar. Cut the bread into 4 thick slices, dip each in water and squeeze out any excess liquid. Add half the quantity of bread to the roe and pound well together. Add the remaining bread according to taste – the less bread you use, the stronger the roe flavour will be. Grate the onion and crush the garlic and add both to the mixture, pounding well. Squeeze the lemon and stir in one tablespoon of juice. Gradually beat in the oil, alternating with another tablespoon of lemon juice. Rub the mixture through a sieve and beat in up to 1 tablespoon milk – this lightens the consistency.

If making in a blender or processor, blend the roe and the bread first with the onion and garlic. Gradually add the lemon juice and oil, blending all the time, and add the milk to lighten. There is no need to sieve in this case.

Pile the mixture into a serving dish and serve immediately with hot pitta bread.

Herring Roe Pâté
TIME 25 minutes plus chilling   SERVES 4   [F]

For those who like a much blander type of pâté, this one has a particularly creamy texture.

8 oz fresh herring roes
1 tablespoon flour
salt and black pepper
6 oz butter
1 large clove garlic
1 dessertspoon lemon juice
nutmeg
2 teaspoons chopped parsley

250 g fresh herring roes
1 tablespoon flour
salt and black pepper
175 g butter
1 large clove garlic
1 dessertspoon lemon juice
nutmeg
2 teaspoons chopped parsley

Wash the roes and pat dry. Sprinkle with flour, mixed with a pinch of salt and a little freshly ground pepper. Heat 2 oz (60 g) of butter in a frying pan. Add the roes to the pan and fry for 5 minutes, turning to cook all sides. Turn into a bowl, including the butter used for frying, and beat well to a paste.

Meanwhile, melt the remaining butter in the pan. Add this gradually to the roes, beating well. Crush the garlic with a little salt and stir in with the lemon juice. Add grated nutmeg and black pepper to taste. Chop the parsley and stir in. Spoon into a small serving dish, cover and chill overnight.

Smoked Salmon Mousse

TIME 25 minutes plus setting   SERVES 6–8   [F]

My favourite luxury starter for a party – and not too outrageous if you use the cheaper smoked salmon pieces. You do need a blender or processor.

¾ pint chicken stock or 1 chicken stock cube	450 ml chicken stock or 1 chicken stock cube
3 tablespoons dry white wine	3 tablespoons dry white wine
½ oz gelatine	15 g gelatine
1 lb smoked salmon pieces	500 g smoked salmon pieces
2 teaspoons lemon juice	2 teaspoons lemon juice
½ pint double cream	300 ml double cream
4 egg whites	4 egg whites

If using a stock cube, boil ¼ pint (150 ml) of water to dissolve and make up to ¾ pint (450 ml) with cold water.

Place the white wine in a bowl over a pan of simmering water, sprinkle on the gelatine and dissolve, stirring occasionally. Meanwhile, pick over the salmon pieces and place in the blender or processor. Mix the stock and the gelatine mixture and gradually add to the salmon, blending until completely puréed. Blend in lemon juice to taste.

Beat the cream until just thick and fold the salmon mixture in. Whisk the egg whites until stiff and fold in gently with a large metal spoon. Pour into a soufflé dish and allow to set for 2 hours or overnight.

Chicken Liver Pâté

TIME 30 minutes plus overnight chilling   SERVES 4   [F]

It is useful to have one meat pâté in your repertoire. You won't
manage a rough-textured terrine in the time, as they need long,
slow cooking, but this is tasty if you like a smooth pâté. You do
need a blender or processor.

2½ oz butter	*70 g butter*
1 small onion (2 oz)	*1 small onion (60 g)*
8 oz chicken livers	*250 g chicken livers*
1 clove garlic	*1 clove garlic*
3 dessertspoons brandy	*3 dessertspoons brandy*
salt and black pepper	*salt and black pepper*
nutmeg	*nutmeg*
2 tablespoons double cream	*2 tablespoons double cream*

Melt ½ oz (15 g) butter in a frying pan. Chop the onion finely and
add to the pan. Cook gently without browning while chopping the
chicken livers and crushing the garlic with a pinch of salt. Add these
to the onions and fry gently for 5 minutes, turning to cook the
livers on all sides.

   Turn into a blender or processor, add the brandy and blend until
smooth. Beat the remaining butter in a bowl until light and creamy.
Beat in the liver mixture and season generously with salt, pepper
and grated nutmeg. Stir in the cream until thoroughly mixed and
spoon into a terrine. Chill overnight.

FISH

We must be the only islanders in the world who are so conservative about fish. Cod, plaice, haddock is our fishy eternal triangle, in spite of the fact that if you blindfolded most people they wouldn't be able to tell one white fish from another, except by texture – and as a nation we mostly eat it smothered in batter, anyway.

Many people have no idea what fresh fish actually tastes like. I accept all that is said about the freezing-at-sea techniques preserving all the nutritional value, but having once in the Isle of Man been served plaice for breakfast at 7 a.m. that had been caught only an hour earlier, I can tell you that it has a delicacy that bears no resemblance whatever to the creature that appears on most fishmongers' slabs, much less in a deep freeze cabinet. So, if you can't have the gourmet experience of morning fresh fish, where individual taste is actually distinguishable, why stick so insistently to the same old varieties?

Maybe as fish becomes more and more expensive, price will make us experiment more willingly. The cheaper coley can look rather grey on its own, but it makes an excellent substitute for cod in made-up dishes, maybe with a cheese or mushroom sauce. And for good flavour, smoked fish or the darker fish – mackerel, herring, trout – have a lot to offer.

Talking of flavour, fish recipes involving a sauce are greatly improved if a home-made fish stock is used, although this is usually only practicable if you have a local wet fish shop. You can substitute the stock wherever water is used – to make fish and rice dishes like kedgeree and paella for instance – or use it half and half with milk when making a white sauce. All you need is 8 oz (250 g) of fish trimmings – ask for the bits when you have a plaice filleted for instance, or ask the fishmonger for cod heads and scraps. Wash thoroughly and place in a saucepan with a small peeled onion, a bay leaf, a pinch of mixed herbs and a sprig of fresh parsley. Cover with water, bring to the boil and simmer gently for 20 minutes. Do not add salt – it is easier to adjust the seasoning when making the recipes. Skim, strain and use immediately, or cool and freeze for future use.

Quick cooks will certainly find it worth while to learn to love fish, as it cooks in a minimum time. If you prefer fish simply fried, keep a polythene bag of seasoned breadcrumbs in the fridge, dip the fish in beaten egg and shake gently in the bag to coat before cooking. Parsley is used in lots of fish recipes, so always buy more than you think you need, chop it all at once and make up little parcels to keep in the freezer (see page xvii).

The idea that fish is good for the brain has, alas, no foundation. It probably arose from the discovery that fish is high in phosphates and that the brain cells need phosphates – so two and two were put together to make *five*.

Now if some enterprising fish sales manager had thought of promoting fish as an aphrodisiac – then the sales graphs might have shown an altogether different pattern.

The recipes in this chapter include butter, cream and thickened sauces. White fish, of course, is also an important part both of a slimming diet, as it is low in calories, and of a low-cholesterol diet, so you will find other ideas, using appropriate secondary ingredients, in those chapters, too.

Cod in Cider Sauce
TIME 30 minutes   SERVES 4

1½ lbs cod fillet	*750 g cod fillet*
1 medium onion (4 oz)	*1 medium onion (125 g)*
1 bay leaf	*1 bay leaf*
2 sprigs parsley	*2 sprigs parsley*
1 dessertspoon lemon juice	*1 dessertspoon lemon juice*
salt	*salt*
15 fl oz dry cider	*450 ml dry cider*

1 oz butter	30 g butter
1 oz flour	30 g flour
2 tablespoons single cream	2 tablespoons single cream

Cut the fish into 4 equal portions and place them in a pan just large enough to hold them comfortably. Slice the onion and add with the bay leaf, parsley, lemon juice and salt. Pour in the cider, cover, and bring to the boil. Simmer gently for 15–18 minutes, depending on the thickness of the fish.

Strain ½ pint (300 ml) of the fish liquor into a measuring jug. In a small pan, melt the butter and sprinkle in the flour. Stir over a medium heat for 1 minute and gradually add the fish liquor, stirring constantly for 2 minutes until smooth and thickened. Add more liquid if necessary to make a pouring consistency. Remove from the heat, stir in the cream and adjust the seasoning to taste.

Remove any skin from the fish, arrange on a plate with the onion and pour the sauce over.

Cod Steaks with Almond Sauce
TIME 30 minutes   SERVES 4

This combination tastes like a mild fondue, so is for people who like the flavour of cheese and white wine.

1 tablespoon flaked almonds	1 tablespoon flaked almonds
4 cod steaks	4 cod steaks
½ lemon	½ lemon
salt and pepper	salt and pepper
2 oz butter	60 g butter
1 oz flour	30 g flour
10 fl oz chicken stock	300 ml chicken stock
2 tablespoons dry white vermouth	2 tablespoons dry white vermouth
3 oz Edam cheese	90 g Edam cheese
2 heaped tablespoons ground almonds	2 heaped tablespoons ground almonds
1 teaspoon made mustard	1 teaspoon made mustard

Place the flaked almonds on a heatproof plate and grill until golden. Leave to cool.

Sprinkle the fish with lemon juice and salt and pepper to taste, dot with 1 oz (30 g) butter and cook under a medium grill for about 5 minutes each side, depending on the thickness of the fish.

Meanwhile, heat the remaining butter in a saucepan, sprinkle in the flour and stir over a gentle heat for one minute. Gradually add the chicken stock and vermouth, stirring constantly until thick and smooth. Remove from the heat. Grate the cheese and stir in with the ground almonds and mustard. Season to taste.

Place the fish in a serving dish, pour the sauce over and sprinkle with the toasted almonds.

Plaice with Grapes
TIME 25 minutes SERVES 2

2 small plaice or dabs	2 small plaice or dabs
1 small onion	1 small onion
8 fl oz dry white wine	¼ litre dry white wine
1 teaspoon lemon juice	1 teaspoon lemon juice
2 sprigs parsley	2 sprigs parsley
salt and pepper	salt and pepper
4 oz large white grapes	125 g large white grapes
1 oz butter	30 g butter
1 oz flour	30 g flour
2 tablespoons double cream	2 tablespoons double cream

Warm a serving dish and boil 1 pint (600 ml) of water in a kettle.

Place the fish in a deep saucepan. Slice the onion and add to the pan with the wine, lemon juice and parsley. Add enough water so that the liquid just covers the fish. Add a pinch of salt and pepper to taste and simmer gently for 10 minutes until the fish is tender.

Meanwhile, pour boiling water over the grapes, skin, de-pip and halve. Strain the fish liquid into a measuring jug and place the fish on the warmed dish.

Melt the butter in a small saucepan, sprinkle in the flour and stir over a gentle heat for 1 minute. Gradually add 8–10 fl oz (250–300 ml) of the fish liquor, stirring all the time until the sauce thickens. (Add milk to make up the quantity if necessary.) Simmer gently, stirring, for 3 minutes. Stir in the grapes.

Remove from the heat, stir in the cream and adjust the seasoning to taste before pouring over the fish.

Orange Stuffed Plaice
TIME 30 minutes   SERVES 2   [F]

To make this recipe in time, it is necessary to have packets of ready prepared breadcrumbs, cheese and parsley (see page xvii), or prepare them the night before and keep in covered bowls.

2 oz butter	60 g butter
2 oz fresh white breadcrumbs	60 g fresh white breadcrumbs
1 orange	1 orange
1 tablespoon lemon juice	1 tablespoon lemon juice
1 tablespoon chopped parsley	1 tablespoon chopped parsley
salt	salt
4 plaice fillets, skinned	4 plaice fillets, skinned
a little cider or white wine	a little cider or white wine
2 oz grated Cheddar cheese	60 g grated Cheddar cheese

Heat the oven to Gas 6; 400° F; 200° C.

Melt the butter and stir in the breadcrumbs. Grate the orange rind and squeeze the juice. Add both to the breadcrumbs with the lemon uice, parsley and salt to taste.

Place the fish fillets, skinned side down, on a board and spread each with the breadcrumb mixture. Roll up, secure with a wooden cocktail stick, and place in an ovenproof dish just big enough to hold the fish. Pour in enough cider or white wine just to cover the bottom of the dish. Sprinkle the grated cheese over the fish and bake for 15 minutes, or until the cheese is melted and the fish is cooked through.

Haddock in Soured Cream
TIME 30 minutes   SERVES 4

This is one of the recipes where a canister of seasoned flour is useful (see page xviii).

2 eggs	*2 eggs*
2 oz butter	*60 g butter*
4 haddock steaks	*4 haddock steaks*
3 tablespoons flour	*3 tablespoons flour*
salt and pepper	*salt and pepper*
4 oz mushrooms	*125 g mushrooms*
1 oz Cheddar cheese	*30 g Cheddar cheese*
10 fl oz soured cream	*300 ml soured cream*

Warm a shallow ovenproof dish. Hard-boil the eggs. Heat the butter gently in a frying pan. Cut each fish steak into ½-inch (1-cm) slices. Mix 2 tablespoons of flour with a pinch of salt and pepper and toss the fish pieces in it – or simply sprinkle with ready-seasoned flour if you have it. Fry in the butter for 5–6 minutes.

Meanwhile, wipe and slice the mushrooms and grate the cheese. Remove the fish from the pan and place on the warmed dish. Add the mushrooms to the pan and fry for 2 minutes. Remove to the warm dish and heat the grill. Sprinkle the remaining flour into the pan and stir for 1 minute. Lower the heat, stir in the soured cream and heat through without boiling.

Shell and slice the eggs and place on top of the fish and mushroom mixture. Pour the sauce over, sprinkle with cheese and place under the hot grill to brown the top.

Creamed Smoked Haddock

TIME 20 minutes   SERVES 2

Served in 4 small ramekins, this also makes a good starter.

8 oz smoked haddock	*250 g smoked haddock*
¾ pint milk	*450 ml milk*
1 oz butter or margarine	*25 g butter or margarine*
1 oz flour	*25 g flour*
2 oz Cheddar cheese	*50 g Cheddar cheese*
black pepper	*black pepper*

Place the smoked haddock in a saucepan and cover with the milk. Simmer gently for 8–10 minutes, until the fish flakes easily. Meanwhile, grate the cheese. Measure ½ pint (300 ml) of the cooking liquid into a jug. Heat the grill.

   Melt the butter or margarine in a small saucepan, sprinkle in the flour and gradually add the fish liquid, beating until smooth and thick. Remove from the heat, stir in half the cheese and the fish, drained of any remaining liquid. Mix well, season with black pepper, and pour the mixture into a shallow ovenproof dish. Sprinkle with the remaining cheese and grill until the cheese is golden.

Quick Kedgeree

TIME 30 minutes   SERVES 4   [F]

The flavour of kedgeree is improved by cooking the rice in the liquid in which you poach the fish. You can cook the fish the previous night, if you have time, and reserve the liquid. If not, this compromise method produces a tasty result.

12 oz smoked haddock	*350 g smoked haddock*
½ bay leaf	*½ bay leaf*
1 oz butter	*30 g butter*
1 medium onion (4 oz)	*1 medium onion (125 g)*
1 teaspoon curry paste	*1 teaspoon curry paste*

8 oz long grain rice	*250 g long grain rice*
salt and black pepper	*salt and black pepper*
2 eggs	*2 eggs*
½ lemon	*½ lemon*

Boil 2 pints (1·25 litres) of water in a kettle. Place the haddock in a saucepan with the bay leaf and cover with ½ pint (300 ml) of boiling water. Cover and simmer gently for 10 minutes.

Meanwhile, heat the butter in a saucepan, chop the onion finely and fry gently with the curry paste for 3 minutes. Stir in the rice and pour in 8 fl oz (¼ litre) of boiling water. Add ½ teaspoon of salt, stir, and allow to simmer very gently, covered, while hard-boiling the eggs.

Measure 7 fl oz (200 ml) of the fish liquor and add to the rice, with the bay leaf. Stir, cover and simmer gently for a further 10 minutes, or until the liquid is absorbed. Squeeze the lemon. Drain the fish, remove the skin and flake the fish into the rice. Shell and chop the eggs and fold in. Season with black pepper, more salt if necessary and lemon juice to taste.

Herrings in Mustard Sauce
TIME 20 minutes   SERVES 4

8 boned herrings	*8 boned herrings*
2 oz butter	*50 g butter*
5 fl oz chicken stock or	*150 ml chicken stock or*
1 chicken stock cube	* 1 chicken stock cube*
1 tablespoon flour	*1 tablespoon flour*
1 tablespoon Dijon or	*1 tablespoon Dijon or*
tarragon mustard	* tarragon mustard*
5 fl oz soured cream	*150 ml soured cream*
salt	*salt*

Heat the grill and cook the herrings on the skin side first for 4–5 minutes. Turn, dot with 1 oz (25 g) butter and continue to cook for a further 5 minutes until golden.

Meanwhile heat the stock, or 5 fl oz (150 ml) water to dissolve the stock cube. Melt the remaining butter in a small saucepan, sprinkle in the flour and stir over a medium heat for 1 minute. Add the stock gradually, stirring for 2 minutes until thickened. Lower the heat, stir in the mustard and soured cream and heat through without boiling. Add salt to taste and pour over the fish just before serving.

Mackerel with Minted Cucumber
TIME 20 minutes   SERVES 2

2 mackerel, boned	2 mackerel, boned
corn oil	corn oil
salt and black pepper	salt and black pepper
½ cucumber	½ cucumber
1 clove garlic	1 clove garlic
1 tablespoon chopped mint	1 tablespoon chopped mint

Brush the fish with a little oil and sprinkle with salt and black pepper. Grill, skin side first, for 5 minutes each side or until beginning to brown.

Meanwhile, skin and dice the cucumber and crush the garlic with a little salt. Heat 1 tablespoon of oil in a frying pan and sauté the cucumber and garlic over a moderate heat, stirring frequently, for 5–8 minutes, or until golden. Chop the mint and add, with salt and pepper to taste.

Place the fish on a serving dish and spoon the cucumber on top.

Prawns and Peppers
TIME 25 minutes   SERVES 2

This dish has pleasing contrasts in colour and fish texture. It can be served as a main course with rice, in which case put the rice on to cook first. Otherwise it makes an attractive starter if served in scallop shells.

3 sticks of celery	*3 sticks of celery*
1 red pepper	*1 red pepper*
1–2 oz butter	*30–60 g butter*
6 oz cod steak	*175 g cod steak*
1 tablespoon flour	*1 tablespoon flour*
salt and black pepper	*salt and black pepper*
2 oz peeled prawns	*60 g peeled prawns*
2 oz small button mushrooms	*60 g small button mushrooms*
1 tablespoon brandy	*1 tablespoon brandy*
1 tablespoon chopped parsley	*1 tablespoon chopped parsley*

Warm a serving plate. Wash and chop the celery. De-seed and dice the pepper. Heat 1 oz (30 g) butter in a sauté pan. Meanwhile cut the cod steaks into 1-inch (2-cm) squares and toss in the flour, seasoned with a little salt and pepper. Add to the pan with the prawns and sauté in the butter for 3 or 4 minutes, until the fish is beginning to brown. Remove to the warm plate. While the fish is cooking, wipe the mushrooms and remove the stalks.

Add the remaining butter to the pan if necessary, add the celery and peppers with a little salt and sauté, stirring, for 2 minutes. Add the mushrooms and continue to cook, stirring, for 2 more minutes. The celery and pepper should remain crisp.

Remove the vegetables to the serving dish. Pour off most of the butter and pour in the brandy, swirling round the pan. Return the vegetables and fish to the pan, toss in the brandy for 1 minute to heat through, adjust the seasoning and serve immediately sprinkled with parsley.

Prawns Creole Style
TIME 25 minutes   SERVES 2

This is one of the few recipes where I feel it is justified to add 'optional' for the garlic. The word used to be included in recipes as a concession to conservative British taste, but garlic is now very much more widely accepted. In this case, if you are very keen on garlic it makes a good mixture, but I think it kills the flavour of the prawns. Try it both ways to discover which you prefer.

2 oz butter	*60 g butter*
1 large onion (6 oz)	*1 large onion (175 g)*
3 sticks celery	*3 sticks celery*
1 large green pepper	*1 large green pepper*
12 oz tomatoes	*350 g tomatoes*
1 clove garlic (optional)	*1 clove garlic (optional)*
1 tablespoon chopped parsley	*1 tablespoon chopped parsley*
salt and pepper	*salt and pepper*
6 oz peeled prawns	*175 g peeled prawns*
Tabasco sauce	*Tabasco sauce*

Boil 1½ pints (900 ml) of water in a kettle. Meanwhile, heat 1½ oz (40 g) butter gently in a sauté pan. Chop the onion finely, add to the pan and cook over a low heat for 3 minutes. Chop the celery and add to the pan. De-seed and dice the pepper and add. Mix well. Continue to cook while preparing the tomatoes.

Place the tomatoes in a bowl and pour over the boiling water. Skin, chop and add, with crushed garlic if used, to the other vegetables. Chop the parsley and add with salt and pepper to taste. Continue to cook gently while heating the remaining butter in a small saucepan.

Toss the prawns in the remaining butter and when heated through add to the vegetables. At this stage the tomatoes should be soft and the green peppers still just crisp. Stir in Tabasco sauce to taste and serve immediately.

Fish Thermidor

TIME 25 minutes   SERVES 4

You can use any thick white fish fillets or steaks for this dish, but if you have a fresh fish shop near, try to get monkfish. It has a slightly chewy texture, which makes it suitable as a lobster substitute.

3 oz butter	*75 g butter*
2 oz flour	*50 g flour*
½ pint fish stock (see page 26)	*300 ml fish stock (see page 26)*
½ pint milk	*300 ml milk*
2–3 tablespoons dry white wine	*2–3 tablespoons dry white wine*
1–1½ teaspoons dried tarragon	*1–1½ teaspoons dried tarragon*
½ teaspoon ready-made English mustard	*½ teaspoon ready-made English mustard*
2 tablespoons grated Emmenthal cheese	*2 tablespoons grated Emmenthal cheese*
1 lb monkfish, or solid white fish	*500 g monkfish, or solid white fish*
1 tablespoon brandy	*1 tablespoon brandy*

Melt 2 oz (50 g) of the butter in a small saucepan and sprinkle in the flour. Stir over a gentle heat for 1 minute. Gradually stir in the fish stock (or water) and milk, stirring constantly to make a smooth, thick sauce. Stir in the wine, tarragon and mustard. Grate the cheese. Remove the pan from the heat and stir in 1 tablespoon of cheese.

Melt the remaining butter in a large frying pan, cut the fish into 1-inch (2-cm) chunks, and sauté in the butter for about 5 minutes, until cooked through. Swirl in the brandy.

Heat the grill. Stir the fish and juices into the sauce and spoon into 4 scallop shells or ovenproof individual dishes. Sprinkle the remaining cheese over and place under a hot grill until the cheese melts.

Poached Fish in Lemon Sauce

TIME 25 minutes   SERVES 4

1½ lbs haddock or cod fillet	*750 g haddock or cod fillet*
1 small onion (2 oz)	*1 small onion (60 g)*
1 bay leaf	*1 bay leaf*
1 lemon	*1 lemon*
salt and black pepper	*salt and black pepper*
1 oz butter	*25 g butter*

1 oz flour	25 g flour
1 egg yolk	1 egg yolk
2 tablespoons single cream	2 tablespoons single cream

Boil 1 pint (600 ml) of water in a kettle. Skin the fish, cut into 4 portions, place in a saucepan and pour in enough boiling water just to cover the fish. Slice the onion and add with the bay leaf, one slice of lemon, and a pinch of salt. Cover and simmer gently for 10–15 minutes, depending on the thickness of the fish. Meanwhile, squeeze the rest of the lemon and separate the egg. Strain ½ pint (300 ml) of the fish liquid into a measuring jug.

Melt the butter in a small saucepan and sprinkle in the flour. Stir for 1 minute over a gentle heat and gradually add the fish liquor, stirring constantly until thick and smooth. Remove from the heat and beat in the egg yolk, cream and finally the lemon juice. Adjust the seasoning to taste. Place the fish on a serving dish and pour the sauce over.

Curried Fish with Peppers
TIME 25 minutes   SERVES 4

4 cod or haddock steaks	4 cod or haddock steaks
salt and pepper	salt and pepper
1 lemon	1 lemon
2 fl oz stock, cider or wine	60 ml stock, cider or wine
1½ oz butter	40 g butter
1 medium onion (4 oz)	1 medium onion (125 g)
1 red pepper	1 red pepper
1 oz flour	30 g flour
½ pint milk	300 ml milk
6 oz Gouda cheese	175 g Gouda cheese
2 dessertspoons curry powder	2 dessertspoons curry powder

Place the fish steaks in a large saucepan and sprinkle with salt and pepper to taste. Squeeze the lemon juice and pour into the pan with enough stock, cider or wine to cover.

Heat ½ oz (15 g) butter in a frying pan, slice the onion and fry without browning for 3 minutes. Meanwhile de-seed the pepper and cut into strips. Add to the onion and cook for another 3 minutes. Spoon the mixture over the fish, cover and simmer gently for 10 minutes.

Meanwhile, grate the cheese. Melt the remaining butter in a small saucepan, sprinkle in the flour and stir over a medium heat for 1 minute. Gradually add the milk, stirring constantly until the sauce is thick and smooth. Simmer, stirring for 3 minutes. Remove from the heat and add 4 oz (125 g) grated cheese and the curry powder, beating until smooth. Heat the grill. Strain a little of the fish juices into the sauce – a tablespoon or two to make it an easy pouring mixture, not too thin. Adjust seasoning to taste.

Place the fish steaks in a heatproof dish, topped with the onions and peppers, and pour the sauce over. Sprinkle with the remaining cheese and place under the hot grill for 2 or 3 minutes, until brown and bubbling.

Trout with Almonds
TIME 25 minutes   SERVES 4

Clarifying butter sounds like a lot of trouble, but it is very useful for quick cooks who rely on a sauté pan, as ordinary butter burns so easily. You can make it and keep it in the fridge for other occasions, but this fish recipe and the following one, which are well known on restaurant menus, incorporate the clarifying in the preparation time, which is my reason for including them.

6 oz butter	175 g butter
4 trout, cleaned and trimmed	4 trout, cleaned and trimmed
seasoned flour (page xviii)	seasoned flour (page xviii)
4 oz blanched almonds	125 g blanched almonds
1–2 teaspoons lemon juice	1–2 teaspoons lemon juice

Warm a serving dish. Melt the butter in a frying pan, then heat without browning until it stops bubbling. Remove from the heat, allow to settle and skim. Pour the liquid butter into a measuring jug, leaving any sediment behind. Wipe the pan clean.

Pour half the butter back into the pan and re-heat. Dust the trout with seasoned flour and fry in the butter for 5–6 minutes each side. Remove to the warm dish. Add the remaining butter to the pan and fry the almonds for 2 or 3 minutes until golden. Stir in the lemon uice (don't overdo it) and pour over the fish.

Skate in Black Butter
TIME 25 minutes   SERVES 4

Like the previous recipe, this one uses clarified butter.

4 small wings of skate	4 small wings of skate
1 onion (4 oz)	1 onion (125 g)
2 tablespoons vinegar	2 tablespoons vinegar
salt	salt
4 oz butter	125 g butter
1 tablespoon chopped parsley	1 tablespoon chopped parsley

Place the skate in a sauté pan, or a saucepan large enough to hold it in one layer. Slice the onion and add. Cover with water and add 1 tablespoon vinegar and half a teaspoon salt. Bring to the boil and simmer for 15–20 minutes while preparing the butter. Chop the parsley.

Place the butter in a small saucepan. Heat gently until it stops bubbling. Skim and pour off the butter into a measuring jug, leaving the sediment behind. Wipe out the pan. Return the butter to the pan and heat until it becomes a rich brown. Do not allow it to become actually black, or it will be burned.

Drain the fish and place it on a serving dish. Sprinkle with the chopped parsley and pour the butter over. Add another tablespoon of vinegar to the pan which contained the butter and swirl it round. Pour this over the fish, too, and serve immediately.

Fish Salad with Tarragon
TIME 30 minutes   SERVES 4

Fish is rarely served cold in this country – apart from in Italian restaurants as an hors d'oeuvre. But it makes excellent salad, either as a starter or as a main course.

1½ lbs cod fillet	750 g cod fillet
salt and black pepper	salt and black pepper
4 fl oz dry white wine	125 ml dry white wine
4 fl oz water	125 ml water
1 tablespoon chopped fresh tarragon	1 tablespoon chopped fresh tarragon
1 clove garlic	1 clove garlic
4 fl oz mayonnaise	125 ml mayonnaise
1 tablespoon lemon juice	1 tablespoon lemon juice
1 red pepper	1 red pepper
lettuce	lettuce

Place the fish in a saucepan with a pinch of salt and cover with the wine and water. Bring to the boil and poach, according to the thickness, for 7–10 minutes, or until the fish flakes. Meanwhile, chop the tarragon and crush the garlic with a little salt. Add both to the mayonnaise with the lemon juice.

Drain the fish liquid into a jug and add 2 tablespoons to the mayonnaise with black pepper and more salt if necessary. Place the fish in a bowl, removing any skin and bone. If you want to eat the dish immediately, spread the fish on a plate to cool quickly. Otherwise fold it gently into the mayonnaise and chill overnight.

De-seed and chop the pepper and fold in just before serving on a bed of lettuce.

Fish with Green Mayonnaise
TIME 30 minutes   SERVES 4

1½ lbs cod fillet
salt and black pepper
4 oz leaf spinach, fresh or
    thawed (8 oz of fresh
    spinach gives about 5 oz of
    stripped leaves)
2 tablespoons chopped onion
1 large clove garlic
1 tablespoon olive oil
1 tablespoon wine vinegar
6 tablespoons mayonnaise
4 tablespoons single cream
lemon juice
4 tomatoes

750 g cod fillet
salt and black pepper
125 g leaf spinach, fresh or
    thawed (250 g of fresh
    spinach gives about 150 g of
    stripped leaves)
2 tablespoons chopped onion
1 large clove garlic
1 tablespoon olive oil
1 tablespoon wine vinegar
6 tablespoons mayonnaise
4 tablespoons single cream
lemon juice
4 tomatoes

Place the cod fillet in a pan with a pinch of salt and cover with water. Bring to the boil and poach gently for 7 minutes or until the fish flakes. Drain and spread on a plate to cool.

If using fresh spinach, strip and wash the leaves and place them in a blender or processor. Chop the onion roughly, crush the garlic with a little salt, and add both to the spinach. Add the oil and vinegar and blend until smooth. Add the mayonnaise and cream and blend again. Stir in a squeeze of lemon juice and add salt and black pepper to taste. If the mixture is too thick, add a little more cream and/or vinegar, to taste. The mixture should be like a thick mayonnaise.

Add the fish to the mixture, fold in carefully, pile on a dish and surround with sliced tomatoes.

Mint and Cucumber Fish Salad

TIME 30 minutes   SERVES 4

1½ lbs cod fillet	750 g cod fillet
½ lemon	½ lemon
salt and black pepper	salt and black pepper
½ cucumber	½ cucumber
2 tablespoons chopped mint	2 tablespoons chopped mint
2 tablespoons chopped parsley	2 tablespoons chopped parsley
¼ teaspoon French mustard	¼ teaspoon French mustard
1 tablespoon wine vinegar	1 tablespoon wine vinegar
3 tablespoons olive oil	3 tablespoons olive oil
lettuce	lettuce
4 tomatoes	4 tomatoes

Skin the fish and cut into 3 or 4 pieces. Squeeze the lemon and place in a pan with the fish, a pinch of salt and enough water to cover. Bring to the boil and simmer gently for 7–10 minutes. Remove the fish and place on a plate to cool quickly.

Peel and dice the cucumber and place in a bowl. Chop the mint and parsley and add. Place ¼ teaspoon salt, pepper and mustard in a small jar and add the vinegar and oil. Shake until well blended and pour over the cucumber. Fold in the fish and turn gently until well coated. Adjust the seasoning and serve on a bed of lettuce, decorated with quartered tomatoes.

POULTRY AND MEAT

I am very old-fashioned about meat. Not, I hope, about the way I cook it, but about the quality of the raw product. Wherever I have lived, I have sought out the best butcher and been totally loyal to him, seeking his advice, trusting his judgement. This has usually meant paying top prices, but I would rather eat meat less often than waste my efforts on tough old beasts that should have been pensioned off.

When supermarkets first went into the fresh meat market, they really didn't compete with the local butcher in terms of quality and variety of cuts, but they have improved tremendously since those early days. One area in which they beat the butcher is in chicken chopping, or the packaging of poultry – turkey, too – as separate joints. You can now buy packets of fresh poultry breasts, thighs, legs, usually in fours and sixes, and graded into similar sizes. All of which makes life for the cook in a hurry much simpler, because such joints cook through conveniently at exactly the same time and you have no need to juggle about putting chicken breasts in after the legs to avoid dryness. Obviously, you have to pay for this privilege, and it is much cheaper to buy a whole chicken and cut it up yourself. If you have no poultry shears, buy your chickens from a butcher and ask him to joint them for you.

Poultry shears are really worth having so that you are never at a loss. You may have a whole chicken which you intended to roast, and then find you have less time than you thought. With your own poultry shears you can joint it quite simply by cutting off the whole legs and slitting the flesh along the breast bones and gradually cutting off the breasts in two whole pieces.

Always cut the legs into two, at the joint between the leg and thigh – or remember to ask your butcher to do this, otherwise the usual practice is to present you with whole legs. Unless you divide them into leg and thigh, they will not cook through at the joint in 30 minutes.

As an average sized chicken serves 4 people, and a big one, 6, you can either use all the pieces in a sauté recipe, or keep the breasts for another meal. One point to remember when keeping chicken is that a cut-up bird deteriorates more quickly when raw than a whole one, so you should not keep it for more than two days in the fridge if it is jointed. It has been said many times, but is always worth repeating, that great care must be taken with frozen chickens and turkeys. They *must* be completely thawed before you begin cooking.

One or two recipes are included for leftover poultry. Families who demolish a roast chicken at one sitting will wonder who has leftovers, but it is surprising how far scraps will go when made into a pilaf, and everybody can always do with a new idea for dolling up cold turkey. Cold turkey and chicken are, of course, interchangeable in all the recipes which specify leftovers. In any case, not all cold bird is leftover. The ready-cooked chickens and chicken portions available are great stand-bys for quick cooks.

A word about veal. A friend tried to persuade me not to include veal in this book because she objects so strenuously to the way it is raised. I do not think that my avoidance of the subject would materially decrease the purchase of veal and as I am a fervent supporter of variety in the kitchen, I have included one or two recipes because veal is a quick-cook meat. However, I do support the view that animals should be raised with as little cruelty as possible, and if you feel strongly about the subject I suggest that in order to make producers change their ways you go and lobby where it counts and not take the line of least resistance by simply not buying veal.

Chicken with Cider and Apples
TIME 30 minutes   SERVES 4

4 chicken joints	*4 chicken joints*
1½ tablespoons corn oil	*1½ tablespoons corn oil*
4 rashers back bacon	*4 rashers back bacon*

1 large onion (6 oz)	*1 large onion (175 g)*
4 Cox's apples	*4 Cox's apples*
4 fl oz cider	*125 ml cider*
½ lemon	*½ lemon*
1 teaspoon sugar	*1 teaspoon sugar*
salt and pepper	*salt and pepper*
1 level tablespoon cornflour	*1 level tablespoon cornflour*
¼ pint single cream	*150 ml single cream*

Brush the chicken joints with ½ tablespoon of oil and cook under a medium grill for 10–12 minutes each side, or until cooked through. Warm a plate at the same time. Meanwhile, heat the remaining oil in a sauté pan, cut the bacon into 1-inch (2-cm) strips and fry until just crisp. Chop the onion.

Remove the bacon to the warm plate, add the onion to the pan and fry gently for 3 minutes without browning. Meanwhile peel, core and slice the apples thickly. Add these to the pan with the cider. Squeeze the lemon juice and add with the sugar and salt and pepper to taste. Simmer for 7–10 minutes or until the apple is soft, but still retains its shape.

Return the bacon to the pan. Blend the cornflour with the cream, stir in and heat through without boiling, adding a little more cider if the sauce is too thick. Adjust the seasoning and pour over the chicken.

Chicken Breasts in Vermouth

TIME 20 minutes   SERVES 2

½ oz butter	*15 g butter*
1 tablespoon corn oil	*1 tablespoon corn oil*
1 tablespoon flour	*1 tablespoon flour*
salt and pepper	*salt and pepper*
2 chicken breasts	*2 chicken breasts*
1 medium onion (about 4 oz)	*1 medium onion (about 125 g)*
¼ pint chicken stock or 1 chicken stock cube	*150 ml chicken stock or 1 chicken stock cube*

3 tablespoons dry white	3 tablespoons dry white
vermouth	vermouth
½ teaspoon dried tarragon	½ teaspoon dried tarragon
2 tablespoons double cream	2 tablespoons double cream
1 dessertspoon chopped parsley	1 dessertspoon chopped parsley

Warm a serving dish. Meanwhile heat the butter and oil in a sauté pan. Dust the chicken breasts with flour mixed with a pinch of salt and a little pepper and fry gently for about 3 minutes on each side. Meanwhile slice the onion and boil a little water to dissolve the stock cube.

Remove the chicken and place on the warm serving dish. Add the onion to the pan and cook gently for 3 minutes. Crumble the stock cube into the pan and add ¼ pint (150 ml) boiling water, or add the homemade stock. Add the vermouth and tarragon and boil rapidly for 2–3 minutes to reduce by half. Remove from the heat, stir in the cream and add salt and pepper to taste. Pour over the chicken breasts and sprinkle with parsley.

Chicken Breasts with Ham

TIME 20 minutes   SERVES 4

1 oz butter	30 g butter
4 chicken breasts	4 chicken breasts
salt and pepper	salt and pepper
4 thin slices cooked ham	4 thin slices cooked ham
4 oz Cheddar cheese	125 g Cheddar cheese

Melt the butter in a frying pan. Place greaseproof paper over the chicken breasts and flatten slightly with a rolling pin. Sprinkle with a little salt and pepper and brown quickly in the butter for 2 minutes. Turn, lower the heat, and cook for 5 minutes more.

Meanwhile heat the grill and grate the cheese. Place the chicken breasts on an ovenproof dish and place a slice of ham on each, trimming the edges of the ham to fit. Sprinkle each with cheese, place under the hot grill and cook for 2 minutes until the cheese is melted and golden.

Chicken with Walnuts
TIME 15 minutes   SERVES 2

The Chinese method of stir-frying – turning food over and over in hot oil for a very short time – can be applied to several types of meat. I use a non-stick pan and two wooden spoons to do the turning.

2–3 tablespoons corn oil	*2–3 tablespoons corn oil*
1 small onion (2 oz)	*1 small onion (60 g)*
2 oz walnut pieces	*50 g walnut pieces*
2 chicken breasts	*2 chicken breasts*
1 dessertspoon cornflour	*1 dessertspoon cornflour*
salt	*salt*
1 tablespoon dry or medium sherry	*1 tablespoon dry or medium sherry*
1 teaspoon sugar	*1 teaspoon sugar*
1–2 teaspoons soya sauce	*1–2 teaspoons soya sauce*

Warm a serving dish. Heat the oil in a sauté pan and meanwhile chop the onion. Add to the pan and fry gently for 2 minutes. Chop the walnuts roughly, add to the onions, and fry together for 3 minutes while preparing the chicken.

Cut the chicken into ½-inch (1-cm) dice and toss in the cornflour mixed with a small pinch of salt. Use less salt than you would normally, otherwise the soya sauce will overdo the seasoning.

Remove the onions and walnuts to the warm dish. Add an extra tablespoon of oil to the pan if needed and fry the chicken quickly for 2 minutes, turning the pieces all the time. Add the sherry, sugar and soya sauce to taste. Return the walnuts and onions to the pan and fry, stirring, for 1 more minute.

Mustard Chicken
TIME 30 minutes   SERVES 4

4 chicken joints	*4 chicken joints*
salt and black pepper	*salt and black pepper*

corn oil

1 small onion (2 oz)

2 tablespoons Dijon mustard

2 tablespoons made English
mustard

1 teaspoon Worcestershire sauce

½ teaspoon tarragon

3 oz fresh wholemeal
breadcrumbs

1 oz butter

corn oil

1 small onion (60 g)

2 tablespoons Dijon mustard

*2 tablespoons made English
mustard*

1 teaspoon Worcestershire sauce

½ teaspoon tarragon

*90 g fresh wholemeal
breadcrumbs*

30 g butter

Heat the grill. Brush the chicken joints with oil and sprinkle with salt and black pepper. Grill for 5 minutes each side.

Meanwhile, grate the onion into a bowl and stir in the mustards, Worcestershire sauce and tarragon, with a small pinch of salt. Grate the breadcrumbs onto a flat plate. Melt the butter.

Place the chicken joints on a board and spread both sides with the mustard mixture. Dip into the breadcrumbs and pat in evenly. Melt the butter and dribble over the joints. Replace under the grill and cook for a further 5–8 minutes each side until the coating is a crusty brown and the chicken cooked through.

Chicken in Wine Sauce

TIME 30 minutes   SERVES 4

1½ oz butter

1 tablespoon corn oil

4 chicken joints

salt and black pepper

2 tablespoons brandy

8 fl oz dry white wine

3 egg yolks

8 fl oz single cream

1 tablespoon chopped parsley

8 oz noodles (optional)

40 g butter

1 tablespoon corn oil

4 chicken joints

salt and black pepper

2 tablespoons brandy

¼ litre dry white wine

3 egg yolks

¼ litre single cream

1 tablespoon chopped parsley

250 g noodles (optional)

If you wish to serve this recipe with noodles, put on a pan of water now and add the noodles while the white wine is simmering.

Heat the butter and oil in a lidded sauté pan. Sprinkle the chicken joints with a little salt and pepper, cover and fry gently for 15 minutes, turning once.

Pour the brandy into the pan, warm through and ignite. Shake the pan until the flames subside and add the white wine. Cover and simmer for 10 minutes. (If serving noodles put them into the boiling water.) Chop the parsley and beat the egg yolks with the cream. Remove the pan from the heat, pour in the cream mixture and mix well with the juices. Return to a very low heat and stir until heated through and slightly thickened. Do not boil. Place the chicken on a serving dish, adjust the seasoning in the sauce, pour over and sprinkle with parsley.

Chicken Livers in Marsala
TIME 30 minutes   SERVES 4   [F]

3 oz butter	75 g butter
1 medium onion (4 oz)	1 medium onion (125 g)
8 oz mushrooms	250 g mushrooms
½ pint chicken stock or 1 chicken stock cube	300 ml chicken stock or 1 chicken stock cube
1–2 tablespoons Marsala	1–2 tablespoons Marsala
2 teaspoons tomato purée	2 teaspoons tomato purée
1 teaspoon arrowroot	1 teaspoon arrowroot
Worcestershire sauce	Worcestershire sauce
salt and pepper	salt and pepper
1 tablespoon corn oil	1 tablespoon corn oil
12 oz chicken livers	350 g chicken livers
2 tablespoons flour	2 tablespoons flour

Boil ½ pint (300 ml) water, if using a stock cube. Heat 2 oz (50 g) butter in a saucepan. Meanwhile chop the onion finely, add to the pan and cook gently for 3 minutes without browning.

Meanwhile wipe the mushrooms and slice. Add to the pan and

cook for a further 3 minutes. Crumble the stock cube into the pan and add the boiling water. Or add the home made stock. Stir in the Marsala and boil rapidly to reduce slightly. Stir in the tomato purée.

Mix the arrowroot with a little water to make a thin cream and stir in. Add Worcestershire sauce and salt and pepper to taste and simmer until required.

Meanwhile, heat the remaining butter with the oil in a sauté pan. Toss the chicken livers in the flour mixed with a little salt and pepper. Sauté the livers in butter quickly until brown on all sides – not more than 2 minutes. Add the mushroom mixture to the pan and adjust the seasoning to taste.

Chillied Chicken Livers with Rice

TIME 25 minutes   SERVES 4

12 oz long grain rice	350 g long grain rice
salt and black pepper	salt and black pepper
1 tablespoon corn oil	1 tablespoon corn oil
1 large onion (8 oz)	1 large onion (250 g)
6 tomatoes	6 tomatoes
2 oz butter	60 g butter
12 oz chicken livers	350 g chicken livers
1 tablespoon flour	1 tablespoon flour
4 oz mushrooms	125 g mushrooms
1 teaspoon chilli powder	1 teaspoon chilli powder
2 tablespoons sherry	2 tablespoons sherry

Boil 2 pints (1·25 litres) of water in a kettle. Measure 22 fl oz. (660 ml) into a saucepan and add the rice with 1 teaspoon of salt. Cook according to the quick method on page 75.

Meanwhile, heat the oil in a small saucepan, chop the onion and fry gently for 5 minutes. Cover the tomatoes with boiling water, skin, chop roughly and add to the onions with a pinch of salt. Cover and simmer gently until required.

Heat the butter in a frying pan, halve the chicken livers and toss in the flour, seasoned with a little salt and black pepper. Add to the butter and sauté for 5 minutes. Meanwhile, wipe and slice the mushrooms, add to the livers and fry for a further 2 minutes. Add the chilli powder (more if you like it hot) and sherry and simmer for a further 5 minutes.

Stir the tomato mixture into the livers and mushrooms, adding a little stock or water if too thick. Adjust the seasoning and serve on the rice.

Spiced Chicken Pilaf
TIME 30 minutes   SERVES 4   [F]

Chicken and turkey are interchangeable when it comes to using the leftovers. Or, if you are really pushed, you can buy ready-cooked joints.

½ oz butter	*15 g butter*
1 medium onion (4 oz)	*1 medium onion (125 g)*
½ teaspoon curry paste	*½ teaspoon curry paste*
10 oz long grain rice	*285 g long grain rice*
8 whole cardamoms	*8 whole cardamoms*
4 whole cloves	*4 whole cloves*
ground cinnamon	*ground cinnamon*
½ teaspoon coriander	*½ teaspoon coriander*
½ teaspoon cumin seeds	*½ teaspoon cumin seeds*
salt and pepper	*salt and pepper*
4 oz frozen peas	*125 g frozen peas*
8 oz cooked chicken	*250 g cooked chicken*
2 oz sultanas	*50 g sultanas*
2 oz whole blanched almonds	*50 g whole blanched almonds*

Boil 18 fl oz (550 ml) of water in a kettle. Heat the butter in a large saucepan. Chop the onion finely and fry gently for 3 minutes with the curry paste. Add the rice and mix well. Add the boiling water, stir and allow to bubble gently, uncovered, until the liquid is just bubbling on the surface.

Meanwhile, add the cardamoms, cloves, a small pinch of cinnamon, the coriander, cumin and 1 teaspoon of salt. All this will take about 15 minutes. Stir in the peas, cover and simmer for a further 10 minutes.

Remove any skin from the chicken, dice the flesh and mix with the sultanas. Place the almonds on a heatproof plate and grill until golden. Add the chicken and sultanas to the rice and continue to simmer for a further 5 minutes. Adjust the seasoning and fold in the almonds just before serving.

Stuffed Turkey Rolls
TIME 30 minutes   SERVES 4

4 turkey steaks	*4 turkey steaks*
1 tablespoon flour	*1 tablespoon flour*
salt and pepper	*salt and pepper*
4 slices cooked lean ham	*4 slices cooked lean ham*
1 oz butter	*30 g butter*
1 tablespoon corn oil	*1 tablespoon corn oil*
4 oz Cheddar cheese	*120 g Cheddar cheese*
3 large tomatoes	*3 large tomatoes*
2 oz walnuts	*60 g walnuts*

Place the turkey on a board and sprinkle with flour mixed with a little salt and pepper. Beat with a rolling pin until thin and twice the size – use more flour if necessary to keep them from sticking. Place a slice of ham on each.

Heat the butter and oil in a frying pan. Boil 1 pint (600 ml) water in a kettle. Grate the cheese and use half the quantity to sprinkle on the ham. Roll the turkey up and secure with wooden cocktail sticks. Fry in the butter and oil over a medium heat for 10 minutes, turning to cook all sides.

Meanwhile, place the tomatoes in a bowl, cover with the boiling water, skin and dice. Chop the walnuts. Heat the grill. Place the turkey rolls in an ovenproof dish and sprinkle with the remaining cheese. Top with the tomatoes and walnuts, sprinkle with a little salt and grill until the cheese melts and the tomato softens.

Chicken and Almond Curry

TIME 25 minutes   SERVES 4

I do not suggest that curries made from leftovers can pretend to be the real thing in which long cooking amalgamates the flavours. But you can achieve a tasty imitation when you feel like something spicier than just cold chicken.

12 oz long grain rice	*350 g long grain rice*
salt	*salt*
2 tablespoons corn oil	*2 tablespoons corn oil*
2 large onions (each 6 oz)	*2 large onions (each 175 g)*
1 tablespoon curry paste	*1 tablespoon curry paste*
1 tablespoon flour	*1 tablespoon flour*
1 chicken stock cube	*1 chicken stock cube*
1 dessertspoon vinegar	*1 dessertspoon vinegar*
12 oz cooked chicken	*350 g cooked chicken*
4 oz small button mushrooms	*125 g small button mushrooms*
8 oz frozen peas	*250 g frozen peas*
2 oz whole blanched almonds	*50 g whole blanched almonds*
5 fl oz soured cream	*150 ml soured cream*

Boil 2 pints (1·25 litres) of water in a kettle. Measure 22 fl oz (650 ml) into a saucepan, add the rice and 1 teaspoon of salt and cook according to the quick method on page 75.

Meanwhile, heat the oil in another saucepan, chop the onions and fry gently for 3 minutes. Add the curry paste and flour and stir for 1 minute. Crumble the stock cube into the pan and stir in the vinegar and 16 fl oz (½ litre) of boiling water. Dice the chicken and add. Simmer gently for 10 minutes. Meanwhile wipe the mushrooms and add to the pan with the peas. Simmer for a further 5 minutes.

Meanwhile heat the grill, place the almonds on a heatproof plate and grill until golden. Remove the curry from the heat, stir in the soured cream and almonds and serve with the rice.

Turkey in Red Wine
TIME 30 minutes   SERVES 4

Turkeys seem to come in more manageable sizes these days, but when I was learning to cook they always seemed to be monsters and we were ploughing through cold cuts until New Year. This was a favourite way of dressing it up with an assortment of other leftovers. You can also make it with cold chicken, in which case you may need a stock cube.

¼ pint turkey stock or 1 chicken stock cube	*150 ml turkey stock or 1 chicken stock cube*
8 oz streaky bacon	*250 g streaky bacon*
2 medium onions, each 4 oz	*2 medium onions, each 125 g*
1 oz butter	*30 g butter*
1 clove garlic	*1 clove garlic*
salt and pepper	*salt and pepper*
1 rounded tablespoon flour	*1 rounded tablespoon flour*
½ pint leftover red wine	*300 ml leftover red wine*
mixed herbs	*mixed herbs*
1 tablespoon redcurrant jelly	*1 tablespoon redcurrant jelly*
4 oz small button mushrooms	*125 g small button mushrooms*
12–16 oz cold turkey	*350–500 g cold turkey*

Heat the stock, or boil ¼ pint (150 ml) water in a kettle to dissolve the stock cube. Chop the bacon into 1-inch (2-cm) pieces and fry in a saucepan large enough to hold all the ingredients. Meanwhile, chop the onion and when the bacon is nearly crisp, add to the pan with the butter. Crush the garlic with a little salt and add. Cook gently for 2 more minutes.

Sprinkle the flour into the pan and mix well. Add the wine and stir for 2–3 minutes, until thickened. Crumble in the stock cube and add ¼ pint (150 ml) boiling water, or add the hot turkey stock. Stir in a very small pinch of mixed herbs and the redcurrant jelly.

Dice the turkey and wipe the mushrooms. Add both to the sauce, season to taste and simmer gently for 15 minutes.

Veal with Almonds

TIME 20 minutes   SERVES 2

2 oz whole blanched almonds	60 g whole blanched almonds
2 oz mushrooms	60 g mushrooms
8 oz escalope of veal, ½ inch thick	250 g escalope of veal, 1 cm thick
2 tablespoons corn oil	2 tablespoons corn oil
1 tablespoon chopped onion	1 tablespoon chopped onion
½ teaspoon ground ginger	½ teaspoon ground ginger
1 dessertspoon cornflour	1 dessertspoon cornflour
1 tablespoon sherry	1 tablespoon sherry
2 tablespoons chicken stock or half a chicken stock cube	2 tablespoons chicken stock or half a chicken stock cube
salt and pepper	salt and pepper

Heat the grill. Place the almonds on a heatproof plate and toast until golden. Wipe and slice the mushrooms. Cut the veal into 1-inch (2-cm) pieces.

Heat the oil in a large frying pan. Chop the onion and fry gently with the ginger for 3 minutes. Add the veal and fry for 2 minutes more, stirring to cook all sides evenly. Add the mushrooms and fry for 1 minute more.

Sprinkle in the cornflour. Add the sherry and the stock or crumbled stock cube and 2 tablespoons of water. Season to taste with salt and pepper and cook gently for 3–4 minutes. Stir in the toasted almonds just before serving.

Sautéed Veal with Caraway Noodles

TIME 25 minutes · SERVES 2

1½ oz butter	40 g butter
8 oz pie veal	250 g pie veal
1 tablespoon flour	1 tablespoon flour
salt and black pepper	salt and black pepper
1 small onion (2 oz)	1 small onion (60 g)

4 oz button mushrooms	*125 g button mushrooms*
1 teaspoon paprika	*1 teaspoon paprika*
2 fl oz dry white wine	*60 ml dry white wine*
4 oz noodles	*125 g noodles*
1 teaspoon caraway seeds	*1 teaspoon caraway seeds*
2–3 fl oz soured cream	*60–80 ml soured cream*

Put a pan of water on to boil for the noodles. Warm a plate. Gently heat 1 oz (30 g) butter in a sauté pan. Meanwhile, remove all the fat from the veal, cut into 1-inch (2-cm) squares and toss in flour with a little salt and black pepper. Add to the pan and sauté for 5 minutes or until browned on all sides and tender inside. Remove to the warm plate.

Chop the onion and add to the pan. Cook gently while wiping and slicing the mushrooms. Add these to the pan with the paprika and sauté for 2 minutes. Add the white wine and reduce the heat.

Add a teaspoon of salt and the noodles to the boiling water and cook for 5–8 minutes, until just tender. Drain, add the remaining butter and the caraway seeds and mix well. By this time the wine will have almost evaporated. If not, raise the heat to reduce. Remove from the heat, add the veal and swirl in the soured cream. Heat through, without boiling, and serve with the noodles.

Beef with Red Peppers
TIME 30 minutes   SERVES 2

The amount of meat here may seem mean, but it is amazing how far it stretches in this type of recipe. You can, of course, use better quality steak if you wish. Based on the stir-fry principle, this dish can be served with rice, in which case put the rice on to boil at the beginning of the recipe.

6 oz braising steak	*175 g braising steak*
1 dessertspoon cornflour	*1 dessertspoon cornflour*
1 dessertspoon soya sauce	*1 dessertspoon soya sauce*
2 tablespoons corn oil	*2 tablespoons corn oil*

1 small onion (2 oz)	*1 small onion (60 g)*
1 stick celery	*1 stick celery*
1 red pepper	*1 red pepper*
½ green pepper	*½ green pepper*
2 tablespoons chicken stock or	*2 tablespoons chicken stock or*
1 chicken stock cube	* 1 chicken stock cube*
2 tablespoons sherry	*2 tablespoons sherry*
salt and pepper	*salt and pepper*

Warm a serving dish and boil ½ pint (300 ml) water in a kettle if using a stock cube. Remove any gristle and fat from the steak and cut it, across the grain, into thin strips 1½ inches × ¼ inch (4 cm × 1 cm). Place on a plate and sprinkle with cornflour and soya sauce. Mix well. Dissolve the stock cube in the boiling water.

Heat the oil in a sauté pan and chop the onion. Fry gently in the oil for 2 minutes without browning. Chop the celery finely, add to the pan and fry for 1 minute. De-seed and chop the peppers, add and fry, stirring, for a further 2 minutes. Remove all the vegetables to the warm dish.

If necessary, add a further tablespoon of oil to the pan. Add the meat and stir-fry for 1 minute only. Return the vegetables to the pan, pour in the 2 tablespoons of chicken stock and the sherry and cook together for 1 minute. Adjust the seasoning and serve immediately.

Budget Stroganoff
TIME 30 minutes   SERVES 4

When good quality steak is so expensive, it seems a terrible waste to do anything to it that might disguise the flavour of the meat. So I never make stroganoff with the fillet specified in the original recipe. Working on the Chinese stir-fry principle, I use good quality braising steak (blade, chuck or whatever is best at your particular butcher), cut it into small strips and fry it very quickly. This is one of the few occasions when it is preferable to prepare all the ingredients first, so that the meat is not kept waiting too long.

12 oz long grain rice	*350 g long grain rice*
salt and black pepper	*salt and black pepper*
1 lb top quality braising steak	*500 g top quality braising steak*
1 medium onion (4 oz)	*1 medium onion (125 g)*
6 oz mushrooms	*175 g mushrooms*
1 tablespoon chopped parsley	*1 tablespoon chopped parsley*
2 oz butter	*60 g butter*
1 beef stock cube	*1 beef stock cube*
5 fl oz soured cream	*150 ml soured cream*
Worcestershire sauce	*Worcestershire sauce*

Boil 1½ pints (900 ml) water in a kettle, pour 1 pint (600 ml) into a saucepan and add the rice and 1 teaspoon salt. Cook according to the quick method on page 75. Warm a serving plate.

Cut the meat into matchstick strips about 2 inches × ½ inch (5 cm × 1 cm). Chop the onion finely. Wipe and slice the mushrooms. Chop the parsley.

Heat the butter in a sauté pan and cook the meat quickly to brown all sides – not more than 2 minutes. Remove to the warm plate. Reduce the heat, add the chopped onion to the pan, and cook gently for 3 minutes. Add the mushrooms and cook for a further 2 minutes.

Dissolve the stock cube in the remaining ½ pint (300 ml) boiling water and add to the pan. Boil rapidly for about 2 minutes to reduce. Remove from the heat, return the meat to the pan and stir in the soured cream. Season to taste with salt, black pepper and Worcestershire sauce and heat through gently without boiling. Serve immediately on the rice, and sprinkle with the chopped parsley.

Meatballs in Tomato Sauce with Noodles
TIME 30 minutes   SERVES 4

Ready-chopped parsley and ready-prepared breadcrumbs are helpful for this recipe.

1 clove garlic	*1 clove garlic*
salt and pepper	*salt and pepper*

2 tablespoons corn oil	*2 tablespoons corn oil*
1 lb tomatoes	*500 g tomatoes*
3 tablespoons chopped parsley	*3 tablespoons chopped parsley*
dried oregano	*dried oregano*
1 lb minced beef	*500 g minced beef*
4 oz breadcrumbs	*100 g breadcrumbs*
2 oz grated Parmesan	*50 g grated Parmesan*
1 egg	*1 egg*
12 oz noodles	*350 g noodles*

Boil 1 pint (600 ml) water in the kettle. Crush the garlic with a little salt. Gently heat 1 tablespoon of oil in a small saucepan. Place the tomatoes in a bowl, cover with boiling water, skin and chop roughly. Add to the pan with the garlic, 1 tablespoon of parsley and oregano, salt and pepper to taste. Simmer gently while preparing the meat balls.

Warm a serving dish and put a pan of water on to boil for the noodles. Place the minced beef in a bowl with the breadcrumbs, Parmesan, remaining parsley and salt and pepper to taste. Add the egg and mix well. Flatten the mixture into a cake, divide into 8, and then with floured hands make 32 small balls.

Heat the remaining oil in a large frying pan and cook the meatballs over a medium heat for 5–10 minutes, according to the degree of rareness liked.

While the meatballs are cooking, add the noodles to the pan of boiling water with 1 teaspoon salt and cook for 5–8 minutes, until just tender. Drain and place in the serving dish. Mix the meatballs with the tomato sauce and place on top of the noodles.

Spiced Meatballs

TIME 25 minutes   SERVES 4

3 tablespoons corn oil	*3 tablespoons corn oil*
1 medium onion (4 oz)	*1 medium onion (125 g)*
1 lb minced beef	*500 g minced beef*
1 teaspoon salt	*1 teaspoon salt*

black pepper	*black pepper*
½ teaspoon cumin seeds	*½ teaspoon cumin seeds*
½ teaspoon ground coriander	*½ teaspoon ground coriander*
1 egg yolk	*1 egg yolk*
2 oz pine kernels	*50 g pine kernels*
2 oz sultanas	*50 g sultanas*

Heat 1 tablespoon of oil in a large frying pan. Chop the onion finely and fry gently for 5 minutes. Place the minced meat in a bowl with the salt, black pepper to taste, cumin seeds and coriander. Add the onion, egg yolk, pine kernels and sultanas and mix well together.

Flour the hands and form teaspoons of the mixture into small balls. Heat the remaining oil in the same frying pan and fry the meatballs for about 10 minutes or until well browned.

Caraway Pork

TIME 30 minutes   SERVES 2

1 oz butter	*30 g butter*
2 oz mushrooms	*50 g mushrooms*
½ teaspoon caraway seeds	*½ teaspoon caraway seeds*
6 oz lean pork steak or fillet	*175 g lean pork steak or fillet*
1 tablespoon flour	*1 tablespoon flour*
salt and pepper	*salt and pepper*
½ pint chicken stock or 1 chicken stock cube	*300 ml chicken stock or 1 chicken stock cube*
2 tablespoons single cream	*2 tablespoons single cream*

Boil ½ pint (300 ml) water if using a stock cube. Heat the butter in a saucepan. Meanwhile, wipe and slice the mushrooms, add to the pan and cook with the caraway seeds for 2 minutes.

Cut the pork into 1-inch (2-cm) strips and toss in the flour mixed with a little salt and pepper. Add to the pan and fry quickly on all sides for 1 minute. Add the chicken stock, or crumble in the stock cube and add the boiling water. Cover and simmer for 15 minutes. Remove from the heat and stir in the cream.

Honeyed Pork Chops

TIME 25 minutes   SERVES 2

1 small onion (2 oz)	*1 small onion (60 g)*
2 tablespoons honey	*2 tablespoons honey*
2 tablespoons wine vinegar	*2 tablespoons wine vinegar*
Worcestershire sauce	*Worcestershire sauce*
2 thick pork chops	*2 thick pork chops*
salt	*salt*

Heat the grill. Chop the onion finely and place in a small saucepan with the honey, vinegar and a dash of Worcestershire sauce. Heat until the honey melts. Rub the chops with salt and place them on a shallow ovenproof dish that will fit your grill pan.

Pour the honey sauce over the chops and grill under a medium heat for about 10 minutes each side, basting regularly. Serve with any remaining juices poured over.

Pork Chops with Apples

TIME 30 minutes   SERVES 2

1 clove garlic	*1 clove garlic*
2 pork chops, each ¾ inch thick	*2 pork chops, each 2 cm thick*
salt and pepper	*salt and pepper*
1 tablespoon corn oil	*1 tablespoon corn oil*
2 dessert apples	*2 dessert apples*
3 tablespoons dry cider	*3 tablespoons dry cider*
3 tablespoons chicken stock or	*3 tablespoons chicken stock or*
½ chicken stock cube	*½ chicken stock cube*

Crush the garlic and rub into both sides of the chops. Scrape off. Sprinkle the chops with salt and pepper on both sides. If using a stock cube, boil ¼ pint (150 ml) water in a kettle.

Heat the oil in a frying pan and cook the chops over a medium heat for 5–8 minutes each side according to thickness. Peel, core and slice the apples. Warm a serving dish.

Push the chops to one side of the pan and add the apple slices. Cook for a further 10–12 minutes, turning the apples to brown all sides. Pour off any remaining fat and place the chops on the serving dish, topped with the apples. Add the cider to the pan and mix well with any brown sticky bits left in the pan. Add the stock, or crumbled stock cube and boiling water, and bring to the boil. Boil quickly for 3–5 minutes until reduced to a thick sauce. Pour over the chops and serve immediately.

Pork Chops in Orange Sauce
TIME 30 minutes   SERVES 4

corn oil	corn oil
4 pork chops	4 pork chops
1 orange	1 orange
½ pint orange juice	½ pint orange juice
1 oz demerara sugar	25 g demerara sugar
½ teaspoon ground ginger	½ teaspoon ground ginger
1 teaspoon arrowroot	1 teaspoon arrowroot

Grease a frying pan with a little oil and fry the chops for about 8–10 minutes on each side. Meanwhile, grate 1 teaspoon of orange rind, peel the orange and divide it into segments. Place the rind in a small pan with the orange juice, sugar and ginger. Simmer for 10 minutes.

Blend the arrowroot with a little water to make a thin cream and add to the orange juice mixture.

Drain any surplus fat from the chop pan, leaving any crusty bits. Add the orange sauce and segments, mix well, cover, and simmer for 5 minutes before pouring over the chops.

Brandied Pork with Noodles
TIME 25 minutes   Serves 4

1 tablespoon corn oil	1 tablespoon corn oil
1 medium onion (4 oz)	1 medium onion (125 g)

6 oz small button mushrooms	*175 g small button mushrooms*
1 oz butter	*30 g butter*
12 oz pork steak or fillet	*350 g pork steak or fillet*
1 tablespoon flour	*1 tablespoon flour*
salt and pepper	*salt and pepper*
3 Cox's apples	*3 Cox's apples*
10–12 oz noodles	*300–350 g noodles*
1 tablespoon brandy	*1 tablespoon brandy*
1 tablespoon white wine	*1 tablespoon white wine*
1 tablespoon chopped parsley	*1 tablespoon chopped parsley*
4–6 tablespoons single cream	*4–6 tablespoons single cream*

Warm a serving dish. Put a pan of water on to boil for the noodles. Heat the oil in a sauté pan. Chop the onion and fry gently in the oil for 3 minutes. Meanwhile, wipe the mushrooms. Add to the onions and fry for a further 2 minutes. Remove to the warm dish.

Heat the butter in the same pan. Cut the pork into small pieces, 1 inch × ½ inch (3 cm × 1 cm), and toss in the flour seasoned with salt and pepper. Fry in the butter, stirring, for 2 minutes. Remove to the warm dish with a slotted spoon, leaving the butter in the pan.

Peel, core and slice the apples and sauté quickly in the butter. Add the noodles to the boiling water with a teaspoon of salt, stir and bring back to the boil. Cook for 5–8 minutes. Warm the brandy in a ladle, ignite and pour over the apples, shaking the pan until the flames die out. Return the pork and vegetables to the pan and pour in the wine. Cook gently until the noodles are tender. Chop the parsley. Remove the pork from the heat, stir in the cream and parsley and serve with the drained noodles.

Paprika Pork

TIME 30 minutes   SERVES 4

¼ pint chicken stock or 1 chicken stock cube	*150 ml chicken stock or 1 chicken stock cube*
12 oz pork fillet	*350 g pork fillet*

1 rounded tablespoon flour | *1 rounded tablespoon flour*
2 teaspoons paprika | *2 teaspoons paprika*
salt and pepper | *salt and pepper*
1½ oz butter | *40 g butter*
1 medium onion (4 oz) | *1 medium onion (125 g)*
¼ pint dry white wine | *150 ml dry white wine*
2 oz small button mushrooms | *50 g small button mushrooms*
2–3 tablespoons single cream | *2–3 tablespoons single cream*

Place the chicken stock in a pan and bring to the boil. Or, if using a stock cube, boil ¼ pint (150 ml) water in a kettle.   Cut the pork into bite-sized pieces and toss in the flour mixed with the paprika and a pinch of salt. Heat the butter in a sauté pan and fry the pork pieces for 2 minutes. Chop the onion, add to the pan and fry for a further 2 minutes.

Add any flour remaining from the pork pieces and fry for 1 minute. Dissolve the stock cube and stir in, or add the heated stock. Stir in the wine and bring to the boil. Meanwhile, wipe the mushrooms and add with salt and pepper to taste. Cover and simmer gently for 5 to 10 minutes. Remove from the heat and stir in the cream just before serving.

Pork and Pineapple with Beansprouts
TIME 25 minutes   SERVES 4

1 large onion (6 oz) | *1 large onion (175 g)*
2 green peppers | *2 green peppers*
7 oz can pineapple rings | *200 g can pineapple rings*
12 oz pork steak | *350 g pork steak*
1 dessertspoon cornflour | *1 dessertspoon cornflour*
2 tablespoons dry or medium sherry | *2 tablespoons dry or medium sherry*
1 tablespoon soya sauce | *1 tablespoon soya sauce*
3 tablespoons corn oil | *3 tablespoons corn oil*
1 chicken stock cube or 4 tablespoons chicken stock | *1 chicken stock cube or 4 tablespoons chicken stock*

1 lb beansprouts	*500 g beansprouts*
salt	*salt*
½ teaspoon sugar	*½ teaspoon sugar*

If using a stock cube, boil ½ pint (300 ml) water in a kettle. Warm a serving plate. Chop the onion, de-seed and chop the peppers. Cut the drained pineapple into chunks. Remove any fat from the pork and cut, across the grain, into strips 2 inches × ½ inch (5 cm × 1 cm). Mix the cornflour in a cup with the sherry to make a thin cream and stir in the soya sauce.

Heat 2 tablespoons of oil in a large sauté pan. Fry the onion for 2 minutes. Add the peppers and fry, stirring, for 2 minutes. Remove the vegetables to the warm plate. Dissolve the stock cube in the boiling water.

At this point pour the remaining oil into a large saucepan and heat gently. Add the beansprouts, sprinkle with salt and stir until well mixed with the oil. Give an occasional stir while cooking the pork.

Sprinkle the pork with a little salt, add to the sauté pan and stir-fry for 2 minutes. Return the vegetables to the pan, sprinkle with the sugar, and add the pineapple pieces. Pour in the cornflour mixture, add 2 tablespoons chicken stock and stir for 1 minute more. If necessary add a little more stock to thin. Adjust the seasoning of both the pork and the beansprouts with salt or soya sauce, and serve together.

Lemon Pork with Mushrooms and Noodles
TIME 25 minutes   SERVES 4

12 oz pork fillet	*350 g pork fillet*
1 egg	*1 egg*
3 tablespoons flour	*3 tablespoons flour*
salt and black pepper	*salt and black pepper*
1 tablespoon cooking oil	*1 tablespoon cooking oil*
3 oz butter	*90 g butter*
4 oz mushrooms	*125 g mushrooms*
½ lemon	*½ lemon*

8 oz noodles	*250 g noodles*
2 Cox's apples	*2 Cox's apples*

Boil a panful of water for the noodles. Cut the pork into strips 2 inches × ½ inch (5 cm × 1 cm). Beat the egg and sprinkle the flour seasoned with a little salt and black pepper on a board. Heat the oil and 2 oz (60 g) butter in a sauté pan. Dip the pork strips first in the beaten egg and then in the flour and fry for 5 minutes, turning to cook all sides.

Meanwhile, wipe and slice the mushrooms. Add these to the pan and fry for 2 minutes. Squeeze the lemon and pour the juice into the pan. Add salt and pepper to taste, mixing well. Leave on a low heat.

Heat the remaining butter in another frying pan. Add the noodles to the panful of boiling water with 1 teaspoon of salt and cook for 5–8 minutes. Peel the apples, leaving them whole, core and cut into rings. Fry in the butter for 2 minutes each side.

Arrange the pork and mushrooms in the centre of a ring of drained noodles and top with the apples.

Gammon in Port
TIME 30 minutes   SERVES 2

2 gammon steaks (each 4 oz)	*2 gammon steaks (each 125 g)*
¼ pint chicken stock or ½ a chicken stock cube	*150 ml chicken stock or ½ a chicken stock cube*
2 tablespoons port	*2 tablespoons port*
2 Cox's apples	*2 Cox's apples*
½ oz butter	*15 g butter*
1 level teaspoon arrowroot	*1 level teaspoon arrowroot*
salt and pepper	*salt and pepper*

Heat the grill and cook the gammon steaks for 3 minutes on each side. Meanwhile, place the stock, or ¼ pint (150 ml) water and the stock cube, in a small pan, add the port and bring to simmering point. Peel, core and slice the apples.

Arrange the apples on the gammon, dot with butter and replace under the grill until the apples are soft and beginning to brown. Meanwhile, mix the arrowroot to a cream with 1 tablespoon of water and add to the port mixture. Stir over the heat until thickened. Adjust the seasoning to taste and pour over the gammon and apple.

Ham with Redcurrant Sauce
TIME 25 minutes   SERVES 4

This is based on Cumberland sauce, but as not everyone has port as a regular ingredient, it is made with leftover red wine.

1 orange	*1 orange*
1 lemon	*1 lemon*
8 oz redcurrant jelly	*250 g redcurrant jelly*
4 slices gammon	*4 slices gammon*
1 level dessertspoon arrowroot	*1 level dessertspoon arrowroot*
2 fl oz red wine or port	*60 ml red wine or port*

Boil 1 pint (600 ml) water in a kettle. Heat the grill. Peel the orange and lemon very thinly with a potato peeler and cut the peel into thin strips. Place in a pan and cover with boiling water. Simmer for 5 minutes, then drain.

Squeeze the juice of both fruits. Place the redcurrant jelly in a small pan and heat until melted. Add the juice gradually, stirring. At this point place the gammon under the grill and cook for 3–5 minutes on each side, depending on thickness.

Place the arrowroot in a measuring jug and mix to a thin cream with 1 dessertspoon of cold water. Make up to 2½ fl oz (75 ml) with red wine or port. Pour into the redcurrant mixture and heat to simmering, stirring until thickened and clear. Stir in the peel and serve with the gammon.

Lamb Chops with Swiss Cheese
TIME 25 minutes   SERVES 4

4 lamb chump chops	*4 lamb chump chops*
4 oz Emmenthal or Gruyère cheese	*100 g Emmenthal or Gruyère cheese*
1 clove garlic	*1 clove garlic*
salt	*salt*
½ oz butter	*15 g butter*

Slit each chop horizontally to the bone. Cut 4 small, thick slices of cheese about 1 oz (25 g) each and place in the slits like a sandwich filling. Fold the cheese, if necessary, to fit the pockets exactly. Heat the grill.

Crush the garlic with salt and rub both sides of the chops. Dot with butter and cook under a medium heat for 5–8 minutes each side, depending on the thickness of the chops. Two minutes before the end of the cooking time, spread the chops with any cheese that has melted into the pan, return to the grill and cook until golden.

Lamb with Celery
TIME 25 minutes   SERVES 4

Another dish that can be served alone, or with rice. Vary it sometimes by adding diced pineapple at the end of cooking.

1 large onion (6 oz)	*1 large onion (175 g)*
4 sticks celery	*4 sticks celery*
8 oz mushrooms	*250 g mushrooms*
1 lb leg of lamb, without bone	*500 g leg of lamb, without bone*
3–4 tablespoons corn oil	*3–4 tablespoons corn oil*
2 tablespoons flour	*2 tablespoons flour*
salt and black pepper	*salt and black pepper*
4 tablespoons chicken stock or 1 chicken stock cube	*4 tablespoons chicken stock or 1 chicken stock cube*

4 tablespoons sherry   *4 tablespoons sherry*
Worcestershire sauce   *Worcestershire sauce*

If using a stock cube, boil ½ pint (300 ml) water in a kettle. Warm a
serving dish. Chop the onion, wash and chop the celery into ½-inch
(1-cm) slices. Wipe and dice the mushrooms. Remove any skin and
fat from the lamb and cut into ½-inch (1-cm) chunks.

Heat 2 tablespoons of oil in a 10-inch (26-cm) sauté pan and fry
the onion for 2 minutes. It doesn't matter if it browns slightly. Add
the celery and stir-fry for 2 minutes, then the mushrooms and stir-
fry for 1 minute more. Remove all the vegetables to the warm dish.
Dissolve the stock cube in the boiling water.

Add the remaining oil to the pan. Toss the lamb pieces in flour
with a little salt and pepper. Add the meat to the pan and stir-fry
for 3–4 minutes, until beginning to brown. Return the vegetables
to the pan and add 4 tablespoons chicken stock, and the sherry.
Sprinkle in Worcestershire sauce to taste – be generous. Stir together
for 2 minutes, adjust the seasoning and serve immediately.

Crispy Coated Lamb Cutlets
TIME 20 minutes   SERVES 4

2 oz wholemeal breadcrumbs   *60 g wholemeal breadcrumbs*
1 small onion (2 oz)   *1 small onion (60 g)*
1 teaspoon dried marjoram   *1 teaspoon dried marjoram*
2 oz walnut pieces   *50 g walnut pieces*
salt and black pepper   *salt and black pepper*
1 egg   *1 egg*
1 tablespoon corn oil   *1 tablespoon corn oil*
8 lamb cutlets   *8 lamb cutlets*
1 tablespoon flour   *1 tablespoon flour*

Grate the breadcrumbs and onion into a bowl and mix with the
marjoram. Chop the nuts very finely and add with a small pinch of
salt. Mix well. Beat the egg in a shallow dish.

Heat the oil in a frying pan. Sprinkle the cutlets with salt and
pepper and dust with flour. Dip first into the egg and then into the

crumb mixture. Place in the frying pan, turn down the heat immediately and cook gently for 5 minutes each side. The cutlets should be golden on the outside and pink in the middle.

Lamb Rolls
TIME 30 minutes   SERVES 4

4 slices leg of lamb, ¼ inch thick	*4 slices leg of lamb, 1 cm thick*
salt and black pepper	*salt and black pepper*
thyme	*thyme*
4 slices cooked ham	*4 slices cooked ham*
4 slices Emmenthal cheese	*4 slices Emmenthal cheese*
1 egg	*1 egg*
4 oz fresh white breadcrumbs	*120 g fresh white breadcrumbs*
2 tablespoons corn oil	*2 tablespoons corn oil*
½ oz butter	*15 g butter*

Place the slices of lamb between greaseproof paper and beat with a rolling pin until thin and doubled in size. Season each slice with a pinch of salt and a little pepper and thyme. Place a slice of ham on each and then a slice of cheese. Roll up and secure with wooden cocktail sticks.

Beat the egg and grate the crumbs, if you have none ready-prepared (see page xvii). Heat the oil and butter in a frying pan, dip each lamb roll first in egg and then in breadcrumbs and fry over a medium heat for about 5 minutes on each side, or until the cheese has melted and the lamb is browned.

Lamb's Liver with Orange
TIME 20 minutes   SERVES 4

This dish goes well with noodles, in which case put on a pan of water
to boil at the beginning of the recipe. Or if you prefer, there is
enough time to cook a risotto as an accompaniment. (See menu
section.)

4 fl oz chicken stock or 1 chicken stock cube	*125 ml chicken stock or 1 chicken stock cube*
3 oz butter	*90 g butter*
2 medium onions (each 4 oz)	*2 medium onions (each 125 g)*
1 lb lamb's liver	*500 g lamb's liver*
2–3 tablespoons flour	*2–3 tablespoons flour*
salt and black pepper	*salt and black pepper*
2 oranges	*2 oranges*
1 tablespoon chopped parsley	*1 tablespoon chopped parsley*

Put a plate to warm and heat the stock in a small pan, or boil the
equivalent amount of water. Heat 2 oz (60 g) butter in a sauté pan.
Slice the onions thinly, add to the pan and fry gently for 3 minutes
without browning. Meanwhile, cut the liver into thin strips, 2
inches × ½ inch (5 cm × 1 cm) and toss in the flour seasoned with
a little salt and pepper. Add to the pan and sauté over a medium
heat for 2 or 3 minutes until browned on all sides. Do not overcook.
Remove the liver and onions to the warm plate.

Add the remaining butter to the pan. Peel and segment 1 orange
and add the segments to the butter. Heat through gently. Squeeze
the juice of the remaining orange and add to the pan with the stock
or crumbled stock cube and boiling water. Allow to bubble fast
for 1–2 minutes. Return the liver and onions to the pan, add the
parsley and stir with the juices until well mixed.

Devilled Kidneys
TIME 30 minutes   SERVES 4   [F]

2 oz butter	60 g butter
1 medium onion (4 oz)	1 medium onion (125 g)
6 oz button mushrooms	175 g button mushrooms
8 lamb's kidneys	8 lamb's kidneys
1 oz flour	30 g flour
¼ pint Guinness	150 ml Guinness
1 beef stock cube	1 beef stock cube
1 teaspoon French mustard	1 teaspoon French mustard
1 teaspoon prepared English mustard	1 teaspoon prepared English mustard
1–2 teaspoons Worcestershire sauce	1–2 teaspoons Worcestershire sauce
salt and pepper	salt and pepper
2 tablespoons single cream	2 tablespoons single cream
1 tablespoon chopped parsley	1 tablespoon chopped parsley

Boil ¼ pint (150 ml) water. Melt the butter in a sauté pan. Slice the onion thinly and fry gently for 3 minutes. Meanwhile wipe and slice the mushrooms, add to the pan and cook with the onion while preparing the kidneys.

Halve and core the kidneys and add to the pan. Sprinkle with the flour, stir for 1 minute and add the Guinness gradually. Crumble in the stock cube and add the boiling water. Stir in the mustards, Worcestershire sauce and salt and pepper to taste. Simmer gently for 3–5 minutes, remove from the heat and stir in the cream. Sprinkle with chopped parsley and serve immediately

PASTA AND RICE

These two are absolutely indispensable to quick cooks. You can slave over potatoes if you are really determined, but as simple pastas take between 5 and 12 minutes to cook and rice 20–25 minutes, they are the speediest fillers around. Boil them, season them and toss in a knob of butter and they make a delicious plain accompaniment to all sorts of main courses.

But they certainly need not always be plain. Pasta is a study in itself, but very few people have the storage space or the inclination to go into the niceties of all the different types, although experts will tell you that certain shapes should go with specific sauces and with no other. As a half-hour cook you really haven't time to bother with all that, so you should stick to a few basic shapes – spaghetti, tagliatelle, otherwise known as noodles (the flat ribbon-like ones that cook in the least possible time), and possibly a fancy shape like shells, which is good for salads. There are also all sorts of schools of thought about rice. I have only one simple rule – get something that will guarantee good results and ignore the expense. I find American long grain rice best – Uncle Ben's for preference or Sainsbury's American easy-cook. Failing those, Sherwood's Basmati rice is good. I am not saying that you can't cook other types of rice perfectly if you have the time. But these are the ones that will give good results when you are starting off.

Even so, I use less liquid than the packets usually say. Normally, they suggest a proportion of two to one. I find a little under that gives just as good results and is absorbed in a shorter time – 15 fl oz of liquid to 8 oz (450 ml to 250 g) of rice for instance, or 30 fl oz to 1 lb (900 ml to 500 g). If you are simply cooking rice with water, then the packet instructions to cover and simmer until the liquid is absorbed will probably just make it in the time at your disposal.

But if you are cooking in chicken stock, this always makes the rice stickier and the best quick method is as follows:

QUICK-COOK RICE

Boil the required amount of water to dissolve the stock cubes. Place the stock in an 8-inch (20-cm) saucepan. Add the salt (half the amount recommended if using stock cubes as they are usually salty). Stir in the rice and bring back to simmering. Allow to bubble until the liquid is lying just on the surface of the rice. Stir once, cover, and simmer gently for the remainder of the cooking time, by which time the liquid will be absorbed. You can use this method with plain salted water, too, instead of the stock.

Rice makes a useful leftover, so it is a good idea to cook more than you need. It will fry up the next day with a little onion, or you can dress it while it is still warm to make it into a salad.

Spaghetti with Anchovy Sauce
TIME 25 minutes   SERVES 4

2 cans (each 2 oz) anchovy fillets	2 cans (each 50 g) anchovy fillets
4 tablespoons corn oil	4 tablespoons corn oil
1 lb spaghetti	500 g spaghetti
salt	salt
1 oz butter	25 g butter
3 oz fresh white breadcrumbs	75 g fresh white breadcrumbs
chilli powder	chilli powder

Put a large pan of water on to boil. Meanwhile, drain the anchovy fillets and chop into small pieces. Heat three tablespoons of oil in a small pan, add the anchovies and cook over a gentle heat, mashing occasionally until dissolved.

Add the spaghetti to the pan of boiling water with 1 teaspoon of salt and boil for 10 to 12 minutes until just tender. Meanwhile, grate the breadcrumbs.

Heat the remaining oil and butter in a frying pan and sauté the crumbs until golden. Sprinkle with a pinch of chilli powder. Drain the spaghetti, mix with the anchovies, toss with the breadcrumbs and serve immediately.

Spaghetti with Seafood
TIME 25 minutes   SERVES 4

1½ lbs tomatoes	700 g tomatoes
2 tablespoons corn oil	2 tablespoons corn oil
1 medium onion (4 oz)	1 medium onion (125 g)
2 cloves garlic	2 cloves garlic
1 lb spaghetti	500 g spaghetti
salt	salt
4 oz or ¼ pint cockles	100 g or 150 ml cockles
2 tablespoons chopped parsley	2 tablespoons chopped parsley
black pepper	black pepper
butter	butter

Boil a kettle of water, enough to cover the tomatoes, and put a large pan of water on to boil. Place the tomatoes in a bowl and pour boiling water over. Heat the oil in another saucepan and chop the onion finely. Fry gently for 3 minutes.

Meanwhile, skin and roughly chop the tomatoes and crush the garlic with a little salt. Add both to the onion and simmer over a low heat. Add the spaghetti to the boiling water with 1 teaspoon of salt and boil for 10–12 minutes, until just tender. Place the cockles in a colander and wash under running water for 5 minutes while the spaghetti is cooking.

At this point chop the parsley, if you haven't any ready-chopped in the freezer, and add to the tomato mixture. Add the cockles and heat through. Season with salt and pepper to taste.

Drain the spaghetti, add a knob of butter and stir in the seafood mixture. Serve immediately.

Spaghetti Carbonara
TIME 30 minutes   SERVES 4

4 rashers streaky bacon	*4 rashers streaky bacon*
3 eggs	*3 eggs*
3 egg yolks	*3 egg yolks*
2 tablespoons single cream	*2 tablespoons single cream*
salt and pepper	*salt and pepper*
1 lb spaghetti	*500 g spaghetti*
2 oz butter	*60 g butter*
grated Parmesan cheese	*grated Parmesan cheese*

Heat a large pan of water for the spaghetti. Meanwhile, cut the bacon into matchstick strips and fry until crisp. Beat the whole eggs with the yolks and beat in the cream with salt and pepper to taste.

Add the spaghetti to the boiling water with 1 teaspoon of salt and cook for 10–12 minutes until just tender. Drain in a colander and quickly melt the butter in the same spaghetti pan.

Return the spaghetti to the pan, add the bacon strips and heat through. Remove from the heat and pour in the egg mixture, stirring until the eggs are just scrambled. The heat from the spaghetti will be enough to cook the eggs. If you keep them on the hob they will overcook. Serve immediately with Parmesan cheese.

Spaghetti with Bacon and Mushrooms
TIME 25 minutes   SERVES 4

12 oz bacon	*350 g bacon*
1 medium onion (4 oz)	*1 medium onion (125 g)*
1 lb spaghetti	*500 g spaghetti*
salt and black pepper	*salt and black pepper*
12 oz mushrooms	*350 g mushrooms*
2 oz butter	*60 g butter*
grated Parmesan cheese	*grated Parmesan cheese*

Heat a large pan of water for the spaghetti. Meanwhile, chop the bacon and fry for about 5 minutes until nearly crisp. Chop the onion, add to the bacon and continue to fry for a further 3 minutes.

Add the spaghetti to the boiling water with 1 teaspoon of salt, and simmer for 12–15 minutes until just tender. Slice the mushrooms. Add the butter to the bacon pan and stir in the mushrooms. Fry, stirring, for 3 minutes.

Drain the spaghetti, return to the pan and fold in the bacon and mushroom mixture. Season with black pepper to taste. Serve with grated Parmesan.

Spaghetti al Pesto
TIME 25 minutes   SERVES 4

This is quite my favourite pasta dish and I just wish basil had a longer season in this country. But it hasn't – and you simply can't make this dish with dried basil. I grow mine in pots specially to have a September feast. You can pound it by hand, but it takes less oil than when using a blender or processor.

1 lb spaghetti	*500 g spaghetti*
salt	*salt*
1 large bunch basil, giving	*1 large bunch basil, giving*
2 oz leaves when stripped	* 60 g leaves when stripped*
2 oz pine kernels	*60 g pine kernels*
1 large clove garlic	*1 large clove garlic*
1 oz Parmesan cheese, grated	*30 g Parmesan cheese, grated*
2–4 fl oz olive oil	*60–120 ml olive oil*
butter	*butter*

Heat a large pan of water to boiling. Add the spaghetti with a teaspoon of salt and cook, uncovered, for 12–15 minutes, until just tender. Meanwhile strip the basil leaves.

By hand: pound the basil in a mortar with the pine nuts. Crush the garlic with a little salt and add with the Parmesan. Gradually add about 2 fl oz (60 ml) olive oil, pounding constantly until you get a thick purée.

By blender or processor: Place the basil in the blender or processor with the pine nuts, garlic, Parmesan and 2 fl oz (60 ml) olive oil. Blend until smooth. Gradually add 1–2 fl oz (30–60 ml) more oil until a thick but not runny consistency is obtained. Add salt to taste.

Drain the spaghetti, add a small knob of butter, and stir in the pesto sauce.

Noodles with Spinach
TIME 25 minutes   SERVES 4   [F] *

Another version of a green sauce for pasta when basil is out of season. It is a lovely bright green. You need a blender or processor.

1 lb fresh spinach	*500 g fresh spinach*
1 lb noodles	*500 g noodles*
2 cloves garlic	*2 cloves garlic*
1 teaspoon salt	*1 teaspoon salt*
4 fl oz corn oil	*120 ml corn oil*
1 tablespoon grated Parmesan	*1 tablespoon grated Parmesan*
1 oz walnuts	*30 g walnuts*

Put a large pan of water on to boil. Pick the leaves off the branches of spinach, wash and place in a colander. Now put the noodles in the boiling water with 1 teaspoon salt and boil for 5–8 minutes.

Place the spinach leaves in the blender or processor. Crush the garlic with the salt and add. Gradually pour in the oil, blending until smooth. Add the Parmesan and the nuts and blend again briefly.

Drain the noodles and return to the pan. Pour in the spinach sauce, mix well over a gentle heat to warm through, and serve immediately.

* The sauce will freeze, not the noodles.

Noodles with Prawns and Cream

TIME 25 minutes   SERVES 4

This is ample as a main course – half the quantity is sufficient as a starter for 4 people. It is also excellent made with diced, boiled ham instead of prawns.

2 oz butter	*60 g butter*
1 small onion (2 oz)	*1 small onion (60 g)*
6 oz button mushrooms	*175 g button mushrooms*
8 oz peeled prawns	*250 g peeled prawns*
2 teaspoons dried dill	*2 teaspoons dried dill*
1 lb noodles	*500 g noodles*
12 fl oz double cream	*350 ml double cream*
2 dessertspoons tomato purée	*2 dessertspoons tomato purée*
salt and pepper	*salt and pepper*
grated Parmesan	*grated Parmesan*

Put a large pan of water on to boil. Melt the butter in a large frying pan. Chop the onion and cook gently in the butter for 5 minutes without browning. Meanwhile, wipe and slice the mushrooms. Add to the pan with the prawns and dill and cook gently for another 5 minutes.

Place the noodles in the pan of boiling water, add 1 teaspoon salt and cook for 5–8 minutes or until just tender. Meanwhile, turn the heat under the frying pan very low and stir in the cream and tomato purée. Add salt and pepper to taste. Do not allow to boil.

Drain the noodles and return to the pan. Stir in the prawn and cream mixture and toss gently. Serve with Parmesan cheese.

Tagliatelle with Chicken Livers

TIME 30 minutes   SERVES 4

2 tablespoons corn oil	*2 tablespoons corn oil*
1 large onion (6 oz)	*1 large onion (175 g)*
1 clove garlic	*1 clove garlic*

salt and pepper	*salt and pepper*
4 oz chicken livers	*125 g chicken livers*
8 oz mushrooms	*250 g mushrooms*
4 tomatoes	*4 tomatoes*
1 tablespoon tomato purée	*1 tablespoon tomato purée*
1 tablespoon freshly chopped	*1 tablespoon freshly chopped*
basil or pinch dried thyme	* basil or pinch dried thyme*
12 oz tagliatelle	*350 g tagliatelle*
grated Parmesan cheese	*grated Parmesan cheese*

Boil 1 pint (600 ml) water to cover the tomatoes and heat a large pan of water for the tagliatelle. Heat the oil in a sauté pan, chop the onion finely and fry gently for 5 minutes. Crush the garlic with a little salt and halve the chicken livers. Add both to the pan and cook for 3 minutes. Wipe and slice the mushrooms, add to the pan and cook for 5 minutes more.

Meanwhile, put the tomatoes in a bowl and cover with boiling water. Skin, chop roughly and add to the pan with the tomato purée. Add the herbs, salt and pepper to taste and simmer until required.

Add the tagliatelle with 1 teaspoon of salt to the pan of boiling water and boil for 5–8 minutes, until just tender. Drain, place in a serving dish and top with the chicken liver sauce. Serve with grated Parmesan cheese.

Tagliatelle with Walnuts
TIME 20 minutes   SERVES 4

2 oz butter	*50 g butter*
1 large onion (6 oz)	*1 large onion (175 g)*
1 clove garlic	*1 clove garlic*
salt and black pepper	*salt and black pepper*
4 oz cooked ham	*125 g cooked ham*
2 oz walnut pieces	*50 g walnut pieces*
8 oz tagliatelle	*250 g tagliatelle*
2 tablespoons chopped parsley	*2 tablespoons chopped parsley*

Heat a large pan of water for the pasta. Meanwhile, melt the butter
in a saucepan, chop the onion and fry gently for 3 minutes. Crush
the garlic with a little salt, chop the ham and walnuts and add them
all to the pan. Heat through gently.

Add the tagliatelle to the boiling water with 1 teaspoon of salt
and boil for 5–8 minutes, until just tender. Meanwhile chop the
parsley. Drain the tagliatelle and stir in the walnut and ham mixture
with the parsley and black pepper to taste.

Tagliatelle with Smoked Salmon
TIME 25 minutes   SERVES 4

2 tomatoes	*2 tomatoes*
½ oz butter	*15 g butter*
1 small clove garlic	*1 small clove garlic*
salt	*salt*
12 oz tagliatelle	*350 g tagliatelle*
6 oz smoked salmon pieces	*175 g smoked salmon pieces*
½ pint double cream	*300 ml double cream*

Put a large panful of water on to boil for the tagliatelle. Boil
enough water in the kettle to cover the tomatoes. Place them in a
bowl, cover with boiling water, skin and chop roughly. Heat the
butter in a small pan and add the tomatoes. Crush the garlic with a
little salt and stir in. Simmer gently for 5 minutes.

Meanwhile, add the tagliatelle to the panful of water and simmer
for 10–12 minutes or until just tender. While they are cooking, cut
the smoked salmon into small strips and add to the tomato mixture
with the cream. Stir until heated through but do not boil.

Drain the tagliatelle, return to the pan and add the smoked salmon
mixture. Turn gently over a low heat and serve immediately.

Tagliatelle with Red Peppers
TIME 20 minutes   SERVES 2

The original Italian recipe suggests grilling the peppers first and removing the skins. If the peppers are really red and ripe though, there isn't any need for this, as they aren't bitter like green peppers.

4 large ripe tomatoes	*4 large ripe tomatoes*
1 tablespoon corn oil	*1 tablespoon corn oil*
1 small onion (2 oz)	*1 small onion (60 g)*
2 red peppers	*2 red peppers*
salt and black pepper	*salt and black pepper*
6 oz tagliatelle	*175 g tagliatelle*

Boil 3 pints (2 litres) of water in a kettle. Place the tomatoes in a bowl and cover with 1 pint (600 ml) boiling water. Pour the remainder into a large pan for the tagliatelle.

Heat the oil in a sauté pan. Chop the onion finely and fry gently for 3 minutes. Meanwhile de-seed and cut the peppers into thin strips, 2 inches (5 cm) long. Add to the pan and fry gently while skinning and chopping the tomatoes. Add these to the pan with salt and pepper to taste and mix well. Simmer gently, stirring occasionally.

Add the tagliatelle to the boiling water with 1 teaspoon of salt. Boil for 5–8 minutes until tender. Drain, add the pepper mixture and toss together.

Wholewheat Macaroni with Mushrooms
TIME 30 minutes   SERVES 2

6 oz wholewheat macaroni	*175 g wholewheat macaroni*
salt and black pepper	*salt and black pepper*
1½ oz butter	*40 g butter*
1 small onion (2 oz)	*1 small onion (60 g)*
1½ oz flour	*40 g flour*
1 pint milk	*600 ml milk*

4 oz button mushrooms	125 g button mushrooms
4 oz Edam cheese	125 g Edam cheese
2 tablespoons chopped parsley	2 tablespoons chopped parsley

Heat the oven to Gas 6; 400° F; 200° C.

Boil 2 pints (1·25 litres) of water in a pan. Add the macaroni with 1 teaspoon salt and simmer for 10 minutes, until just tender.

Meanwhile, heat the butter in a saucepan. Chop the onion finely and fry gently for 3 minutes. Sprinkle in the flour, stir for 1 minute, then gradually add the milk, stirring constantly until smooth and thick.

Wipe and slice the mushrooms and stir into the sauce. Grate the cheese. Remove the sauce from the heat and stir in 2 oz (60 g) of cheese. Chop the parsley and add. Adjust the seasoning to taste. Drain the macaroni, stir in the sauce and turn into a 1½ pint (900 ml) ovenproof dish. Sprinkle with the remaining cheese and place in the oven for 10 minutes until the cheese is golden.

Baked Vermicelli and Tomatoes

TIME 30 minutes   SERVES 2–3

1 lb tomatoes	500 g tomatoes
1 clove garlic	1 clove garlic
salt	salt
2 oz breadcrumbs, white or brown	60 g breadcrumbs, white or brown
8 oz vermicelli	250 g vermicelli
2½ oz butter	75 g butter
1 teaspoon oregano or marjoram	1 teaspoon oregano or marjoram
black pepper	black pepper

Heat the oven to Gas 5; 375° F; 190° C.

Boil a kettle of water, to cover the tomatoes, and put a large pan of water on to boil for the vermicelli. Put the tomatoes in a bowl and pour the boiling water over. Skin and cut into thick slices. Crush the garlic with a little salt. Grate the breadcrumbs.

Place the vermicelli in the pan of water with 1 teaspoon salt and boil for 3 minutes only. Drain, and add ½ oz (15 g) butter and the garlic. Grease a 1½-pint (900-ml) ovenproof dish and sprinkle with half the breadcrumbs. Cover with a layer of tomatoes, sprinkle with half a teaspoon of oregano or marjoram, and season with salt and black pepper to taste. Add half the vermicelli, another tomato and herb layer and top with the remaining vermicelli. Sprinkle the remaining breadcrumbs on the top and dot with the remaining butter. Bake for 15 minutes at the top of the oven until the top is golden and crusty.

Spaghetti with Instant Tomato Sauce
TIME 20 minutes   SERVES 4

Don't attempt this unless you can get really ripe tomatoes – the sauce will not have the correct sweetness. You need a blender or processor.

1 lb spaghetti	*500 g spaghetti*
salt	*salt*
1½ lbs ripe tomatoes	*750 g ripe tomatoes*
1 clove garlic	*1 clove garlic*
1 teaspoon sugar	*1 teaspoon sugar*
2 tablespoons olive oil	*2 tablespoons olive oil*
1 tablespoon chopped parsley or fresh basil (not dried)	*1 tablespoon chopped parsley or fresh basil (not dried)*

Heat a large pan of water for the spaghetti. When boiling, add 1 teaspoon of salt and the spaghetti and boil for 12–15 minutes until tender.

Meanwhile boil 2 pints (1.25 litres) of water in a kettle. Place the tomatoes in a bowl, cover with boiling water and skin. Crush the garlic, put in a blender or processor with the tomatoes and sugar and blend until smooth. Add the oil gradually to make a thick sauce.

Chop the parsley or basil. Drain the spaghetti, stir in the tomato sauce with the parsley or basil and heat through. Serve immediately.

Spaghetti with Tomatoes and Onion
TIME 30 minutes   SERVES 4

1 tablespoon olive oil – a herb-flavoured one is good for this	1 tablespoon olive oil – a herb-flavoured one is good for this
1 medium onion (4 oz)	1 medium onion (125 g)
1½ lbs ripe tomatoes	750 g ripe tomatoes
1 teaspoon chopped parsley	1 teaspoon chopped parsley
salt and black pepper	salt and black pepper
1 teaspoon sugar	1 teaspoon sugar
1 lb spaghetti	500 g spaghetti
small knob butter	small knob butter

Heat the olive oil in a saucepan. Chop the onion and cook gently for 3 minutes without colouring. Meanwhile, boil 2 pints (1·25) of water in a kettle, place the tomatoes in a bowl and cover with boiling water. Skin and chop roughly and add to the pan. Chop the parsley and add with a pinch of salt, a sprinkling of black pepper and the sugar. Cover and simmer for 20 minutes.

Heat a large pan of water for the spaghetti, add 1 teaspoon salt and the spaghetti and cook for 12–15 minutes until tender. Check the tomatoes and if too liquid, uncover and allow to evaporate and thicken. Drain the spaghetti, toss with a knob of butter, stir in the tomato sauce and serve immediately.

Curried Macaroni and Ham Salad
TIME 25 minutes   SERVES 4

8 oz wholewheat macaroni	250 g wholewheat macaroni
salt and pepper	salt and pepper
2 tablespoons wine vinegar	2 tablespoons wine vinegar
1 tablespoon olive oil	1 tablespoon olive oil
4 oz button mushrooms	125 g button mushrooms
6 oz sliced cooked ham	175 g sliced cooked ham
3 tablespoons mayonnaise	3 tablespoons mayonnaise

5 fl oz soured cream	150 ml soured cream
2 tablespoons curry powder	2 tablespoons curry powder
1 bunch watercress	1 bunch watercress
1 oz black olives	25 g black olives

Heat a large pan of water to boiling. Add 1 teaspoon of salt and the macaroni and boil for 10–12 minutes until just tender. Meanwhile, place the vinegar and oil in a large bowl and whisk with a little salt. Wipe the mushrooms, slice and mix with the oil and vinegar. Reserve two slices of ham, cut the remainder into strips and add to the mushrooms. In another bowl, mix the mayonnaise, soured cream and curry powder.

Drain the macaroni in a sieve and rinse in cold water. Drain thoroughly and add to the mushrooms. Stir in the mayonnaise mixture and mix well, adjusting the seasoning to taste.

Arrange the watercress round the edge of a flat serving dish and pile the salad in the centre. Cut the remaining two slices of ham in half, roll up and place on the salad, interspersed with the olives.

Chicken and Prawn Pilaf
TIME 30 minutes   SERVES 4   [F]

A paella is a very splendid and long-winded concoction whose main idea is the combination of meat and shellfish. This simple pilaf uses just two of its ingredients – chicken and prawns.

1 pint chicken stock or 2 chicken stock cubes	600 ml chicken stock or 2 chicken stock cubes
2 tablespoons corn oil	2 tablespoons corn oil
1 large onion (6 oz)	1 large onion (175 g)
1 red pepper	1 red pepper
1 clove garlic	1 clove garlic
salt and black pepper	salt and black pepper
12 oz long grain rice	350 g long grain rice
4 oz cooked chicken	125 g cooked chicken
8 oz cooked prawns	250 g cooked prawns
2 oz black olives	50 g black olives

Heat the chicken stock or, if using stock cubes, bring 1 pint (600 ml) of water to the boil. Heat the oil in a large saucepan. Meanwhile, chop the onion and cook gently in the oil for 3 minutes. De-seed and slice the red pepper and crush the garlic with a little salt. Add both to the pan and mix well. Stir in the rice.

Dissolve the stock cube in the boiling water and add, or pour in the hot chicken stock with a pinch of salt. Allow the liquid to simmer, uncovered, until just bubbling on the surface of the rice. Meanwhile, dice the chicken.

Add the chicken and prawns to the rice, stir and cover. Simmer gently for the remaining 15 minutes, until the liquid is absorbed. Check the seasoning, fold in the black olives and serve immediately.

Mushroom Risotto
TIME 30 minutes   SERVES 4

15 fl oz chicken stock or 2 chicken stock cubes	*425 ml chicken stock or 2 chicken stock cubes*
2 oz butter	*60 g butter*
1 medium onion (4 oz)	*1 medium onion (125 g)*
8 oz long grain rice	*250 g long grain rice*
salt	*salt*
2 oz mushrooms	*50 g mushrooms*
4 oz Cheddar cheese	*125 g Cheddar cheese*

Heat the chicken stock or, if using stock cubes, boil 15 fl oz (425 ml) water. Heat 1 oz (30 g) butter in a saucepan. Chop the onion and cook gently in the butter for 2 minutes without browning. Stir in the rice until well mixed. Add the stock, or dissolve the stock cubes in the water and add. Stir in 1 teaspoon salt (less if using stock cubes, as the cheese is salted, too). Cook according to the quick method on page 75.

Meanwhile, wash and slice the mushrooms and grate the cheese. Just before the end of the cooking time, melt the remaining butter in a frying pan and sauté the mushrooms for 2 minutes. When the rice is ready, remove from the heat and add the mushrooms and cheese. Stir gently until well mixed and serve immediately.

Indian Spiced Rice
TIME 30 minutes   SERVES 4   [F]

This spicy rice, which develops an attractive golden colour during cooking, is an excellent accompaniment to plain grilled fish or meat, which can be easily prepared while the rice is cooking.

22 fl oz chicken stock or 2 chicken stock cubes	*650 ml chicken stock or 2 chicken stock cubes*
1 oz butter	*30 g butter*
1 medium onion (4 oz)	*1 medium onion (125 g)*
1 large clove garlic	*1 large clove garlic*
salt	*salt*
1 teaspoon cumin seeds	*1 teaspoon cumin seeds*
6 whole cardamoms	*6 whole cardamoms*
3 cloves	*3 cloves*
½ teaspoon ground ginger	*½ teaspoon ground ginger*
½-inch cinnamon stick	*1 cm cinnamon stick*
12 oz long grain rice	*250 g long grain rice*

Heat the chicken stock, or boil 22 fl oz (650 ml) water if using stock cubes. Melt the butter in a large saucepan. Meanwhile, chop the onion finely and fry gently in the butter for 3 minutes. Crush the garlic with a little salt and add with the cumin, cardamom, cloves, ginger, cinnamon stick and rice. Mix well until the rice looks transparent.

Dissolve the stock cubes in the boiling water and add. If using home-made stock, stir in 1 level teaspoon salt. Allow to bubble, uncovered, until the liquid is just resting on top of the rice. Cover and continue to simmer until all the liquid is absorbed – about 15 minutes.

Chicken and Rice Salad
TIME 30 minutes   SERVES 6

8 oz long grain rice	*250 g long grain rice*
salt and pepper	*salt and pepper*
5 fl oz whipping cream	*150 ml whipping cream*
5 fl oz mayonnaise	*150 ml mayonnaise*
1 level teaspoon curry powder	*1 level teaspoon curry powder*
2 Cox's apples	*2 Cox's apples*
1 small red pepper	*1 small red pepper*
1 tablespoon chopped parsley	*1 tablespoon chopped parsley*
1 teaspoon lemon juice	*1 teaspoon lemon juice*
12 oz cooked chicken	*350 g cooked chicken*
lettuce	*lettuce*

Measure 15 fl oz (450 ml) of water into a pan and bring to boiling point. Add 1 teaspoon of salt and the rice and cook according to the quick method on page 75.

Meanwhile, whip the cream and fold in the mayonnaise and curry powder. Core the apples (do not peel), dice and add to the mayonnaise mixture. De-seed the pepper, cut into strips and add with the parsley. Add the lemon juice and season to taste.

Turn the rice into a large bowl to cool slightly. Skin the chicken, remove the flesh and dice. Stir into the mayonnaise mixture and finally fold in the rice. By this time the salad should be cold. If required, chill overnight. Serve on a bed of lettuce.

VEGETABLES AND SALADS

For generations vegetables have had, metaphorically, but certainly not literally, a raw deal. Judging by the amount of diligent over-cooking that went on, anyone would think that Boiling for Britain was a competitive sport. But since more people started worrying about their health and started to examine the possibilities of a vegetarian diet – or at least one which includes more imaginative greenery, as opposed to 'rabbit food' – the delights of slightly crisp, undercooked vegetables have been discovered. This chapter is not for those who intend to make vegetables their mainstay. The recipes are not balanced with that purpose in view, but have been devised simply as interesting accompaniments.

Interesting vegetables and salads are, of course, invaluable to quick cooks, as they can turn the simplest grill or cold cut if not into a feast, at least into an attractive stimulant to eye and appetite.

Single people and figure-watchers will have no trouble at all in adapting to the idea of providing one quick-to-prepare vegetable. But if you have a family used to meat and two veg, then you do have a little adjusting to do. It really is not necessary to eat potatoes at every meal – there are plenty of alternatives, including noodles or rice, or even crusty wholemeal rolls, which provide bulk and carbo-hydrate.

If you insist on serving potatoes, remember that it is quicker to scrub them and boil them in their skins than to peel them first. This applies to old potatoes as well as new. The skins come off easily when they're cooked – or you can leave them on, if they aren't discoloured, as most of the nutrition is just under the skin. Jacket potatoes will bake in half an hour, if you use one of those six-armed spikes that go through the middle of the potatoes, and if you don't mind the extra cost involved in using the oven just for them.

To boil old potatoes quickly, cut them into eighths – they will cook in about 10 minutes. If you have time to boil, drain and cool them the night before you need them, you can slice and sauté them in butter or oil when required or mash them into a big potato cake, mixed with seasoning and a little fried onion, and fry in butter until brown on both sides.

Vegetable purées are a useful addition to your repertoire if you have to use frozen vegetables, and however devoted to fresh vegetables you are, it's no good pretending that any but the most fanatical health food addicts don't use the odd frozen pea. Nobody who knows about food pretends that frozen peas taste like fresh ones gathered from the garden, although they are often as good as the sort you can buy from a greengrocer. As good as, but not similar to – the way that instant coffee is all right if you like it for what it is, but it is nothing like real coffee. Nevertheless, nobody could deny the value of frozen vegetables and fruit in a kitchen, particularly out of their normal season. The other vegetables I like to keep in the freezer are those that would normally take a long time to prepare – leaf spinach, green beans, sweet corn.

As a rough guide, if you use fresh vegetables, this is the time it takes me to prepare them:

    1 lb runner beans, string and slice – 10 minutes
    1 lb cabbage, core and shred   – 5 minutes
    1 lb carrots, scrape and dice   – 8 minutes
    2 lbs leeks, wash, slit and slice   – 5 minutes
    2 lbs potatoes, scrub and quarter   – 8 minutes
    1 cauliflower, divide into florets   – 3 minutes
    1 head celery, scrub and slice   – 3 minutes
    4 oz mushrooms, wipe and slice   – 3 minutes

As for salads, the permutations are endless as almost everything goes with everything else. I can't think of any raw vegetable that actually detracts from the flavour of another, so the rule is simply to vary texture and colour as much as possible. But if you haven't a processor to take all the hard work out of chopping and slicing, it is best not to be over ambitious, otherwise the preparation time won't beat the clock. A combination of two or three vegetables is enough to cope with at once.

Another useful habit to adopt is that of cooking more vegetables than you need when you do have the time. A simple French dressing will keep in the fridge in a screw top jar for at least a week – I have kept it much longer, but purists would insist that fresh is best. Cook too many boiled potatoes, too big a cauliflower, too many beans and dress any leftovers while they are still warm, adding a little chopped spring onion. Any of these would make a delicious salad the following day.

All the salads in this section are made with vegetables – main course salads with meat, fish, rice or pasta are to be found in the appropriate chapters.

Broccoli with Almonds
TIME 15 minutes   SERVES 4

Vegetables and nuts are excellent partners. Here's a way of using almonds – or try them with beans, as in the following recipe, or with cauliflower.

1½ lbs broccoli	*750 g broccoli*
salt and black pepper	*salt and black pepper*
2 oz butter	*50 g butter*
2 oz whole blanched almonds	*50 g whole blanched almonds*
1 teaspoon lemon juice	*1 teaspoon lemon juice*

Bring to the boil about 1 inch (2 cm) of water in a large saucepan. Trim the broccoli, discarding the tough ends of the stalks. Add the florets to the water with ½ teaspoon salt. Cover and simmer for 8–10 minutes, or until just tender.

Meanwhile, melt the butter in a large frying pan and fry the almonds until golden. Drain the broccoli, add to the frying pan with the lemon juice and turn in the butter until well mixed. Sprinkle with freshly ground black pepper.

Beans with Almonds

TIME 25 minutes   SERVES 4

The time given in this case assumes the use of fresh beans, which will take 15 minutes to string and slice. If you use whole frozen beans the recipe can be made in 10 minutes.

1½ lbs runner beans or 1 lb frozen whole green beans	750 g runner beans or 500 g frozen whole green beans
salt	salt
2 oz whole blanched almonds	50 g whole blanched almonds
1 oz butter	30 g butter

String and slice the beans, if using fresh ones. Bring to the boil approximately 1 inch of water (2 cm) in a large saucepan. Add the beans with a pinch of salt and boil, covered, for 10 minutes if fresh, 5 minutes if frozen, or until just tender.

Meanwhile, heat the grill, place the almonds on an ovenproof dish and toast until golden. Drain the beans, add the butter and fold in the almonds just before serving.

Green Bean and Potato Purée

TIME 25 minutes   SERVES 4   [F]

This purée is a beautifully bright green. You need a blender or processor.

4 medium potatoes (8 oz when peeled)	4 medium potatoes (250 g when peeled)
salt	salt
12 oz frozen green beans	350 g frozen green beans
1 oz butter	30 g butter
1 tablespoon double cream	1 tablespoon double cream
black pepper and nutmeg	black pepper and nutmeg

In a saucepan, heat enough water to cover the potatoes. Peel the potatoes and quarter. Add to the pan with a pinch of salt, cover and boil for 10–15 minutes until tender. Meanwhile, heat a little water in another pan and when boiling add a pinch of salt and the beans. Simmer for 3–5 minutes until just tender.

Drain the beans and place them in a blender or processor, with the butter. Blend until smooth. Drain the potatoes, add to the beans with the cream, season with salt, pepper and nutmeg to taste, and blend again.

Sweet and Sour Chinese Cabbage
TIME 7 minutes   SERVES 4

1 lb Chinese cabbage	*500 g Chinese cabbage*
1 teaspoon salt	*1 teaspoon salt*
3 teaspoons sugar	*3 teaspoons sugar*
2 tablespoons vinegar	*2 tablespoons vinegar*
2 tablespoons corn oil	*2 tablespoons corn oil*
soya sauce	*soya sauce*

Shred the cabbage thinly. Place the salt in a teacup with the sugar and vinegar. Heat the oil in a large saucepan and add the cabbage. Stir until well mixed with the oil. Sprinkle with a few drops of soya sauce and pour in the vinegar mixture. Cook, uncovered, over a high heat for no more than 2 minutes. The cabbage should be very crisp.

Carrots with Cardamom
TIME 25 minutes   SERVES 4

1½ lbs carrots	*750 g carrots*
1 teaspoon salt	*1 teaspoon salt*
2 oz butter	*60 g butter*
2 oz soft dark brown sugar	*60 g soft dark brown sugar*
rind of 1 orange	*rind of 1 orange*
12 whole cardamoms	*12 whole cardamoms*

Place 8 fl oz (¼ litre) of water in a saucepan and bring to the boil. Meanwhile, peel the carrots and cut into 1-inch (2-cm) strips. Add to the pan with a pinch of salt, cover and cook for 10 minutes.

Meanwhile, melt the butter in a small saucepan with the brown sugar. Grate the orange rind and pound or crush the cardamoms. Add to the butter mixture and heat until the sugar has dissolved.

Drain the carrots, return to the pan and pour in the orange mixture. Adjust the seasoning to taste and mix well.

Carrots in Soured Cream

TIME 25 minutes   SERVES 4

1½ lbs carrots	*750 g carrots*
salt	*salt*
1 tablespoon chopped parsley	*1 tablespoon chopped parsley*
5 fl oz soured cream	*150 ml soured cream*

Heat about 1 inch (2 cm) of water in a saucepan. Meanwhile, scrape the carrots and cut into julienne strips 1 inch × ¼ inch (2 cm × 1 cm). (This takes about 15 minutes.)

Add the carrots to the boiling water with a pinch of salt, cover and simmer for 5 minutes or until just tender. Drain, return to the pan and add the parsley and soured cream. Stir over a very gentle heat until warmed through. Do not allow the cream to boil.

Cauliflower Purée

TIME 25 minutes   SERVES 4

Use a blender or processor for this one, but don't over-blend. A slightly textured purée is better in this case than a perfectly smooth one.

1 large cauliflower	*1 large cauliflower*
salt and black pepper	*salt and black pepper*

1 oz butter
2 tablespoons single cream
nutmeg

30 g butter
2 tablespoons single cream
nutmeg

Heat 1 inch (2 cm) of water in a large saucepan. Meanwhile, divide the cauliflower into florets. Add to the water when boiling with ½ teaspoon of salt. Cover and boil for 10 minutes, or until just tender. Drain and place in the blender or processor. Add the butter and cream and blend. Return to the pan, adjust the seasoning and add grated nutmeg to taste. Heat through gently.

Courgettes and Tomatoes

TIME 15 minutes   SERVES 4

1 tablespoon corn oil
1 large onion (8 oz)
1 lb courgettes
1 clove garlic
salt and black pepper
½ lb tomatoes
1 tablespoon chopped parsley

1 tablespoon corn oil
1 large onion (250 g)
500 g courgettes
1 clove garlic
salt and black pepper
250 g tomatoes
1 tablespoon chopped parsley

Heat the oil in a large saucepan. Slice the onion thinly and cook very gently without browning while preparing the other vegetables. Boil 1 pint (600 ml) water in a kettle.

Wash and trim the courgettes and cut into ½-inch (1-cm) slices. Crush the garlic with a little salt. Place the tomatoes in a bowl, cover with boiling water, skin and chop roughly.

Add the courgettes to the pan and cook for 2 minutes. Add the tomatoes, garlic and parsley, with black pepper and more salt to taste. Cover and simmer gently for 5–8 minutes, until the tomatoes are soft and the courgettes only just tender.

Sautéed Cucumber with Bacon
TIME 25 minutes   SERVES 3–4

This mixture is very good with fish.

8 oz bacon	*250 g bacon*
1 large cucumber	*1 large cucumber*
2 oz butter	*60 g butter*
1 teaspoon sugar	*1 teaspoon sugar*
salt and black pepper	*salt and black pepper*
1 tablespoon chopped parsley	*1 tablespoon chopped parsley*

Heat the grill and cook the bacon until crisp. Meanwhile, peel and halve the cucumber lengthways and scoop out the seeds. Dice the flesh.

Heat the butter in a sauté pan, add the cucumber and sprinkle with the sugar and a little salt and black pepper to taste. Fry lightly for 2 or 3 minutes. Do not allow to become soft.

Chop the parsley and the bacon. Add to the pan and mix well.

Buttered Leeks
TIME 15 minutes   SERVES 4

1½ lbs small even-sized leeks	*750 g small even-sized leeks*
2 oz butter	*60 g butter*
salt and black pepper	*salt and black pepper*
1 tablespoon chopped parsley	*1 tablespoon chopped parsley*

Trim the leeks and cut a long slit lengthways in each. Wash under cold water, fanning out the layers to remove any grit. Cut into 1-inch (2-cm) slices.

Melt the butter in a large sauté pan, add the leeks and sprinkle with salt to taste. Cook over a medium heat for 5–8 minutes, stirring occasionally. Do not cover and don't worry if some of the pieces break up a little. They remain a pretty fresh green and should be quite crunchy. Chop the parsley while they are cooking. Spoon the leeks into a serving dish and sprinkle with the parsley and black pepper to taste.

Savoury Peas
TIME 20 minutes   SERVES 3–4

8 oz frozen peas	*250 g frozen peas*
salt and pepper	*salt and pepper*
1 oz butter	*30 g butter*
4 oz button mushrooms	*125 g button mushrooms*
1 oz flour	*30 g flour*
½ pint cider	*300 ml cider*
4 oz Cheddar cheese	*125 g Cheddar cheese*
2 oz breadcrumbs	*30 g breadcrumbs*

Heat a little water in a saucepan, add the peas with a pinch of salt and simmer for 5 minutes. Meanwhile, melt the butter in another saucepan. Wipe and slice the mushrooms, and fry gently in the butter for 2 minutes. Heat the grill.

Sprinkle the flour onto the mushrooms and stir gently over a medium heat for 1 minute. Add the cider gradually, stirring until thickened. Season to taste.

Drain the peas, add to the sauce and pour into a 1-pint (600-ml) shallow heatproof dish. Grate the cheese, mix with the breadcrumbs, sprinkle over the peas and place under the hot grill until brown and bubbling.

Sprouts with Brazil Nuts
TIME 25 minutes   SERVES 4

1½ lbs Brussels sprouts or 1 lb frozen sprouts	*750 g Brussels sprouts or 500 g frozen sprouts*
salt	*salt*
1 oz butter	*30 g butter*
2 oz Brazil nuts	*60 g Brazil nuts*
cayenne pepper	*cayenne pepper*

Remove the outer leaves and stems of the sprouts. Cut a cross in the stem end. (This helps the thicker part to cook at the same rate as the leafy end.) Half-way through the preparation put water to a depth of 1 inch (2 cm) in a saucepan and bring to simmering.

Place the sprouts in the pan with a pinch of salt, cover and cook for 5–8 minutes, depending on size. They must not become too soft.

Meanwhile, heat the butter in a frying pan and sauté the Brazil nuts until golden. Drain on kitchen paper, sprinkle with cayenne and toss with the drained sprouts just before serving.

Vegetable Medley
TIME 30 minutes   SERVES 4

As the vegetables should remain crisp, this is one of the occasions when the main ingredients should be prepared first, to avoid over-cooking while you chop. If you have a processor all the slicing and dicing can be done in that, which obviously cuts down the time.

1 large onion (8 oz)	*1 large onion (250 g)*
1 lb carrots	*500 g carrots*
4 sticks celery	*4 sticks celery*
1½ oz butter	*40 g butter*
salt and black pepper	*salt and black pepper*
2 oz mushrooms	*50 g mushrooms*
1 tablespoon chopped parsley	*1 tablespoon chopped parsley*

Slice the onion, peel and dice the carrots, chop the celery. Melt 1 oz (30 g) of butter in a deep sauté pan, add the onions and cook gently for 3 minutes without browning. Add the carrots and celery with salt and pepper to taste. Cover and cook, stirring occasionally, for 10–15 minutes, or until the vegetables are nearly tender. If they look as if they might burn, add a very little stock or water, but don't overdo it. While they are cooking, wipe and dice the mushrooms and chop the parsley.

Add the remaining butter and the mushrooms to the pan and cook, uncovered, for a further 2 minutes. Stir in the parsley and adjust the seasoning before serving.

Rösti

TIME 30 minutes   SERVES 4

The original Swiss version of this recipe parboils the potatoes for
10 minutes, then grates them into the pan, but the idea works well
as a way of using up leftover potatoes, too.

1 oz butter	*30 g butter*
1 tablespoon olive oil	*1 tablespoon olive oil*
1 medium onion (4 oz)	*1 medium onion (125 g)*
1 lb cold boiled potatoes	*500 g cold boiled potatoes*
salt and black pepper	*salt and black pepper*

Heat the butter and oil in a 6-inch (15-cm) frying pan. Meanwhile,
skin the onion and chop finely. Add to the pan and fry gently
without browning for 3–5 minutes.

Grate the potatoes coarsely into a bowl and add salt and pepper
to taste. Add the onion and mix gently. Try to keep the potato in
flakes, rather than mashing together. Turn the mixture into the
pan and press lightly to form an even cake. Fry for about 5 minutes
over a medium heat, or until golden brown underneath. Slide onto
a board and turn back into the pan to cook the other side until
golden.

Hot Potato Salad

TIME 25 minutes   SERVES 4

1½ lbs small new potatoes	*750 g small new potatoes*
salt and pepper	*salt and pepper*
4 fl oz mayonnaise (about 8 tablespoons)	*125 ml mayonnaise (about 8 tablespoons)*
1 teaspoon lemon juice	*1 teaspoon lemon juice*
2 teaspoons curry powder	*2 teaspoons curry powder*
2 crisp dessert apples	*2 crisp dessert apples*
2 oz sultanas	*60 g sultanas*

Put enough water to cover the potatoes into a saucepan and bring to the boil. Scrub the potatoes, do not peel, and cut into halves. Add to the pan with 1 teaspoon of salt and boil for 15 minutes, or until tender.

Meanwhile, place the mayonnaise in a large bowl and add the lemon juice and curry powder. Core and dice the apples without peeling and stir in with the sultanas. Drain the potatoes and fold into the mayonnaise mixture. Adjust the seasoning and serve hot.

Candied Sweet Potatoes
TIME 30 minutes   SERVES 4

This is one of the traditional accompaniments to American Thanksgiving turkey. It is also good with lamb chops and veal. Sweet potatoes should normally be peeled after boiling, but dicing them cuts down the cooking time. They may discolour slightly, but the candy coating covers up.

1½ lbs sweet potatoes	*750 g sweet potatoes*
salt	*salt*
2 oz butter	*60 g butter*
4 oz demerara sugar	*120 g demerara sugar*
2 tablespoons water	*2 tablespoons water*

Boil 2 pints of water in a kettle. Peel the sweet potatoes and cut into 1-inch (2-cm) dice. Pour the boiling water into a large pan, add 1 teaspoon of salt and the potatoes, cover and boil for 5–7 minutes, until just tender.

Meanwhile, heat the butter, sugar and water in a 10-inch (26-cm) sauté pan (preferably non-stick), until the sugar dissolves. Drain the potatoes, sprinkle with a little more salt and add to the syrup. Cook over a gentle heat, turning occasionally until the sugar syrup has completely coated the potatoes with a sugar crust – about 10 minutes. Serve immediately.

Potato Cakes
TIME 20 minutes MAKES 10

Next time you are making mashed potatoes, cook an extra three large ones. Then, when the potatoes are cooked and mashed, weigh the required amount and allow to cool.

8 oz cooked mashed potatoes	*250 g cooked mashed potatoes*
2 oz flour	*50 g flour*
salt	*salt*
1 oz butter	*25 g butter*

Place the potatoes in a bowl with the flour. Melt the butter in a large frying pan and pour it all gradually into the bowl, mixing with a fork until smooth, leaving the pan just greased. Add salt to taste.

Turn onto a floured board and roll out to $\frac{1}{4}$ inch (1 cm) thick. Cut into $2\frac{1}{2}$-inch (6-cm) rounds, and fry in batches for 2 minutes each side, or until golden brown. Place on a wire tray to cool slightly, spread with a little butter and serve warm.

Avocado Salad
TIME 15 minutes SERVES 4

2 lemons	*2 lemons*
2 small avocados	*2 small avocados*
2 red apples	*2 red apples*
1 stick celery	*1 stick celery*
2 oz walnuts	*50 g walnuts*
3 tablespoons olive oil	*3 tablespoons olive oil*
salt and pepper	*salt and pepper*
1 head chicory	*1 head chicory*

Squeeze the lemons. Peel and halve the avocados, remove the stones and dice the flesh. Place in a bowl and toss in the lemon juice. Quarter and core the apples, but do not peel. Dice and add to the avocados, mixing gently. Chop the celery and walnuts and add.

Drain off the lemon juice and measure 1 tablespoon into a cup. Add the olive oil, a pinch of salt and pepper and whisk well with a fork. Pour over the salad and toss gently until well mixed. Arrange the chicory on 4 plates and pile the salad in the centre.

Beans Niçoise
TIME 30 minutes   SERVES 4

This can, of course, be made with fresh whole beans, if you have the time to prepare them.

1 lb frozen whole green beans	500 g frozen whole green beans
salt and black pepper	salt and black pepper
lettuce	lettuce
1 clove garlic	1 clove garlic
1 tablespoon wine vinegar	1 tablespoon wine vinegar
3 tablespoons olive oil	3 tablespoons olive oil
1 tablespoon chopped parsley	1 tablespoon chopped parsley
4 firm tomatoes	4 firm tomatoes
2 oz black olives	50 g black olives
2 oz can anchovy fillets	50 g can anchovy fillets

Place the beans in a pan with a pinch of salt and a little water and cook, covered, for about 10 minutes, until tender. Drain and spread on a plate to cool. Meanwhile, wash the lettuce and arrange round the edges of a serving dish.

Crush the garlic with a little salt and place in a bowl large enough to hold all the salad ingredients. Add the vinegar and oil with black pepper and whisk well with a fork. Chop the parsley and stir in.

Quarter the tomatoes and stir into the dressing with the cooled beans and black olives. Add more salt to taste. Arrange in the centre of the serving dish and decorate with the anchovy fillets.

Cabbage Salad
TIME 15 minutes   SERVES 4

1 lb Chinese cabbage	*500 g Chinese cabbage*
1 tablespoon grated onion	*1 tablespoon grated onion*
2 carrots	*2 carrots*
2 sticks celery	*2 sticks celery*
1 oz walnuts	*25 g walnuts*
4 tomatoes	*4 tomatoes*
1 tablespoon wine vinegar	*1 tablespoon wine vinegar*
3 tablespoons corn oil	*3 tablespoons corn oil*
salt and pepper	*salt and pepper*
2 oz sultanas	*50 g sultanas*

Shred the cabbage and place it in a serving bowl. Peel and grate the onion, grate the carrots, chop the celery and walnuts and quarter the tomatoes. Add to the cabbage.

Place the vinegar and oil in a small screw top jar with salt and pepper to taste, and shake together. Pour over the vegetables, add the sultanas and mix together gently to coat all the vegetables with the dressing.

Celeriac and Pepper Salad
TIME 30 minutes   SERVES 4

This combination of white celeriac, red and green peppers and sultanas makes a colourful winter salad.

1 lemon	*1 lemon*
salt	*salt*
1 celeriac root, about 1 lb	*1 celeriac root, about 500 g*
1 red pepper	*1 red pepper*
1 green pepper	*1 green pepper*
1 stick celery	*1 stick celery*
1 tablespoon wine vinegar	*1 tablespoon wine vinegar*

3 tablespoons olive oil	3 tablespoons olive oil
1 Cox's apple	1 Cox's apple
1 oz sultanas	25 g sultanas

Squeeze the lemon juice into a bowl and add a large pinch of salt. Peel the celeriac and cut into matchstick pieces, 1 inch (2 cm) long, adding to the lemon juice as you go along to prevent discolouring. Chill while preparing the other vegetables. De-seed the peppers, cut into strips, and place in another bowl. Scrub the celery, slice finely and add to the peppers.

Place the vinegar and oil with a pinch of salt and a little black pepper in a screw top jar and shake well. Pour over the peppers and celery. Core and dice the unpeeled apple and add.

Drain the celeriac in a sieve and rinse under cold running water. Turn onto kitchen paper and pat dry. Add to the other vegetables with the sultanas and mix well. Serve immediately or chill until required.

Celeriac Rémoulade

TIME 25 minutes   SERVES 4

This is a cross between the authentic French celeri-rave rémoulade, which involves a mustard sauce made with oil, and sauce rémoulade, which is a mayonnaise with capers.

1 celeriac root, about 1 lb	1 celeriac root, about 500 g
1 tablespoon chopped parsley	1 tablespoon chopped parsley
½ pint mayonnaise	300 ml mayonnaise
2 tablespoons French mustard (Dijon with mustard seed is best)	2 tablespoons French mustard (Dijon with mustard seed is best)
1 teaspoon lemon juice	1 teaspoon lemon juice
salt	salt

Boil 1 pint (600 ml) of water in a kettle. Peel the celeriac and cut into matchstick strips about 1 inch (2 cm) long. Immediately place in a saucepan, cover with boiling water and boil for 1 minute only.

Drain, run under the cold tap and place in a bowl. Chop the parsley.

Mix the mayonnaise with the mustard, lemon juice and parsley and fold in the celeriac. Add salt to taste and chill well.

Coleslaw
TIME 10 minutes   SERVES 4

This is a quick salad even by hand, but if you have a processor to do the grating it is as instant as a salad can be.

12 oz white cabbage	*350 g white cabbage*
2 sticks celery	*2 sticks celery*
2 medium carrots	*2 medium carrots*
salt and black pepper	*salt and black pepper*
1 teaspoon sugar	*1 teaspoon sugar*
1 tablespoon wine vinegar	*1 tablespoon wine vinegar*
3 tablespoons corn oil	*3 tablespoons corn oil*
3 tablespoons mayonnaise	*3 tablespoons mayonnaise*
4 tablespoons single cream	*4 tablespoons single cream*

Remove the hard core and outer leaves of the cabbage. Shred finely and place in a large bowl. Scrub the celery and chop finely. Peel and grate the carrots. Add both to the cabbage. Place half a teaspoon of salt and a little black pepper with the sugar in a cup and add the vinegar and oil. Mix well with a fork and pour over the vegetables. In the same cup mix the mayonnaise with the cream until well blended. Add this to the salad and mix well. Add black pepper and more salt to taste and serve immediately or chill until required.

Spinach Salad
TIME 25 minutes   SERVES 4

This is a dish I learned in Arizona. They serve it as a starter, but you could have it as an accompaniment to grilled meat or fish.

4 oz streaky bacon	125 g streaky bacon
4 oz mushrooms	125 g mushrooms
8–12 oz fresh spinach	250–350 g fresh spinach
½ teaspoon salt	½ teaspoon salt
black pepper	black pepper
3 teaspoons wine vinegar	3 teaspoons wine vinegar
2 tablespoons corn oil	2 tablespoons corn oil

De-rind the bacon and fry until crisp. Meanwhile wipe and slice the mushrooms. Remove the bacon from the pan and cool. Add the mushrooms to the bacon fat and fry for 2 minutes.

Wash the spinach and strip the leaves from the stems, removing the centre vein of each leaf if it is tough. Shake dry and tear into small pieces. Place in a bowl.

Mix the salt, pepper, vinegar and oil in a cup, whisking with a fork. Crumble the bacon over the spinach and add the mushrooms and dressing. Toss well together and divide into four individual salad bowls, or serve on side plates.

Red Salad
TIME 15 minutes   SERVES 4

1 lb red cabbage	500 g red cabbage
6 oz cooked beetroot	175 g cooked beetroot
8 large radishes	8 large radishes
salt and black pepper	salt and black pepper
1 tablespoon wine vinegar	1 tablespoon wine vinegar
3 tablespoons corn oil	3 tablespoons corn oil
1 teaspoon caster sugar	1 teaspoon caster sugar

Remove the stalk from the cabbage and shred the leaves finely. Chop across the shreds into small pieces. Place in a bowl. Slice the beetroot and trim and slice the radishes. Add both to the cabbage.

Place ½ teaspoon salt and a little black pepper in a cup and add the vinegar and oil. Whisk well with a fork and whisk in the sugar. Pour over the salad and serve immediately or chill until required.

Hawaiian Rice Salad
TIME 20 minutes plus chilling   SERVES 4

6 oz long grain rice	175 g long grain rice
salt and black pepper	salt and black pepper
1 dessertspoon wine vinegar	1 dessertspoon wine vinegar
3 dessertspoons corn oil	3 dessertspoons corn oil
2 rings of canned pineapple	2 rings of canned pineapple
1 red pepper	1 red pepper
1 banana	1 banana
1 oz sultanas	30 g sultanas
lemon juice	lemon juice

Boil 1 pint water in a kettle. Place the rice in a saucepan with 1 teaspoon salt and add 11 fl oz (325 ml) boiling water. Stir, cover and simmer gently until the liquid is absorbed.

Meanwhile place ½ teaspoon of salt and a little black pepper in a cup and stir in the vinegar and oil. Pour over the cooked rice while still hot. Chop the pineapple, de-seed and dice the pepper, and add both to the rice. Chop the banana and add with the sultanas. Mix well, add a squeeze of lemon juice and adjust the seasoning to taste. Chill for half an hour or overnight.

Grapefruit and Rice Salad
TIME 30 minutes   SERVES 4–6

2 teaspoons salt	2 teaspoons salt
½ teaspoon paprika	½ teaspoon paprika
pepper	pepper
2 tablespoons sugar	2 tablespoons sugar
2 tablespoons lemon juice	2 tablespoons lemon juice
5 tablespoons corn oil	5 tablespoons corn oil
8 oz long grain rice	250 g long grain rice
2 grapefruit	2 grapefruit
1 medium onion (4 oz)	1 medium onion (125 g)
1 green pepper	1 green pepper

Put 15 fl oz (425 ml) of water in a large pan with 1 teaspoon of salt
and bring to the boil. Place the remaining salt in a screw top jar with
the paprika, pepper, sugar, lemon juice and oil. Add the rice to the
pan, and simmer until the water bubbles just on top of the rice.
Then cover and simmer for 15–20 minutes, until the liquid is
absorbed.

   Meanwhile, halve the grapefruit and cut out the segments, discarding the pith and pips. Chop the segments and place in a bowl.
Slice the onion, dice the pepper and add to the grapefruit. Add the
rice when the liquid has been absorbed. Shake the jar until the
dressing is well mixed and pour over the rice while it is still hot.
Toss well. Serve warm or allow to cool until required.

Roquefort Dressing
TIME 5 minutes   SERVES 4

Roquefort can sometimes be a little over-salty and this is an excellent
way of using up this expensive cheese. Or use any other strong blue
cheese. It is best made in a blender or processor. It is delicious with
very crisp, very cold Iceberg lettuce.

2 oz Roquefort cheese	50 g Roquefort cheese
2 oz cream cheese	50 g cream cheese

2 tablespoons wine vinegar	*2 tablespoons wine vinegar*
5 tablespoons corn oil	*5 tablespoons corn oil*
1 small clove garlic	*1 small clove garlic*
1 teaspoon caster sugar	*1 teaspoon caster sugar*
2 tablespoons milk	*2 tablespoons milk*

Place the Roquefort and the cream cheese in the blender or processor. Add the vinegar and half the oil and blend until smooth. Mash the garlic and add with the sugar and the remaining oil. Blend again. Add up to 2 tablespoons of milk, blending continuously, until you achieve the consistency of a thick pouring sauce.

SLIMMERS

There is no such thing as magic food. Whatever you eat turns into you, unless you burn it off again with some sort of exercise. So, if you think you have a weight problem – and that usually means 10 lbs more weight than is shown in those tables of weight-for-height recommended by insurance companies – the best way to control it is to eat less.

You don't need funny foods done up in slimming packs. You don't need expensive food. You do need to eat smaller portions of the foods that are high in calories and to try to keep to an average of 1,200 calories a day. Remember the word average. Most dieters (I have struggled long enough to know) have a built-in, never-on-Sunday mentality. Starting a diet is strictly a Monday morning undertaking and many people think that if they go over the top on Wednesday they can't recoup, so they give up until the following Monday. Not true. Set your calorie allowance and if you eat 200 too many one day, take in 100 less than your allowance for the following two days. It is the weekly total that counts. You may need to keep to 1,000 calories for a while, but you should always ask your doctor's advice before embarking on any strict diet – and don't think you shouldn't 'bother' a busy doctor with questions of weight. Obesity *is* a health hazard.

If you have a weight problem you will find a calorie chart useful. But no one can contemplate calorie counting for a lifetime without collapsing with boredom at the very idea, so here are seven basic rules:

1. Grill, poach and bake, rather than fry.
2. Use less butter or oil.
3. Choose eggs, fish, chicken, kidney and liver more often than beef, lamb, pork and cheese.

4. Purée soups rather than thicken with flour.
5. Use low-fat yogurt instead of cream.
6. Use artificial sweeteners more often than sugar.
7. Remember that all food is fattening. It's how much you eat that counts.

Some diets are worked out on a carbohydrate count and slimmers are told they can eat as much as they like of certain foods. Beware. This only works if you are very overweight. If you find it difficult to lose weight, you will still have to keep your intake down. Bearing this in mind, here are some guidelines for choosing foods least likely to put on weight if eaten in controlled quantities:

Allowed foods: All green vegetables, clear soups, milkless coffee and tea, lean meat, liver, kidney, white fish, shellfish, eggs, cottage cheese, grapefruit and citrus fruits.

Restricted foods: Bread (1 oz slice per day), potatoes (2 small per day), up to 1 pint skimmed milk per day, ½ oz butter or margarine or polyunsaturated margarine per day (they all have the same number of calories per oz unless they say they are specifically a low-calorie spread), fruit (2 pieces per day), Edam cheese (1 oz per day).

Forbidden foods: Cream, cream substitutes, soured cream, fat meat, sausages, peas, all beans except green beans, canned fruit in syrup, bananas, dried fruit, all sugar products – cakes, biscuits, puddings, ice cream, chocolate, sweets, jams, marmalade, honey.

This chapter does not pretend to be a complete guide to losing weight. It simply aims to provide some recipes which are calorie-counted so that you can serve them to the whole family and yet keep an eye on your intake. Who has time to prepare special portions of this and that for figure-watchers? And anyway, living on nothing but plain grilled foods and salad is so depressing. All these dishes can be served without any apologetic murmurings about being on a diet – just add potatoes or other carbohydrate fill-ups for non-slimmers and they need never know they have been served diet food.

If you are keen on combining slimming with lowering your cholesterol count, that's what the next chapter is about.

Watercress Soup

TIME 30 minutes   SERVES 4   [F]
CALORIES PER PORTION 125

This is a very popular soup with non-slimmers, too. You do need
a blender or processor if you are to avoid housemaid's elbow.
Watercress isn't easy to sieve.

1¾ pints chicken stock or 2 chicken stock cubes	1 litre chicken stock or 2 chicken stock cubes
½ oz butter	15 g butter
1 large onion (6 oz)	1 large onion (175 g)
3 medium new potatoes	3 medium new potatoes
2 bunches watercress	2 bunches watercress
salt and black pepper	salt and black pepper

Heat the chicken stock or boil 1¾ pints (1 litre) of water if using
stock cubes. Melt the butter in a large saucepan and chop the
onion. Fry gently in the butter for 3 minutes, without browning.
Meanwhile scrape and dice the potatoes. Add to the onion and cook
for a further 2 minutes.

Wash the watercress, strip the leaves, and add. Dissolve the stock
cube in the boiling water and stir in – or add the hot chicken stock.
Add salt and pepper to taste and simmer gently for 15–20 minutes.

Place in a blender or processor and blend until smooth. Return
to the pan, adjust the seasoning, and serve either hot or cold.

Smoked Haddock Mousse

TIME 30 minutes plus setting   SERVES 6
CALORIES PER PORTION 68

8 oz smoked haddock	250 g smoked haddock
½ oz sachet gelatine	15 g sachet gelatine
3 oz cottage cheese	90 g cottage cheese
1 lemon	1 lemon

black pepper	*black pepper*
2 egg whites	*2 egg whites*

Place the fish in a saucepan and cover with water. Bring to the boil
and simmer for 5 minutes. Measure ¼ pint (150 ml) of the liquid into
a bowl and sprinkle with the gelatine. Set over a small pan of
simmering water and stir occasionally until dissolved.

Meanwhile, remove any bones and skin from the fish and place
in a blender or processor. Sieve the cottage cheese and add. Squeeze
the juice of the lemon and add 1½ tablespoons to the fish with black
pepper to taste. Gradually pour in the gelatine mixture, blending all
the time until smooth. Pour into a bowl and place in the fridge for
5 minutes to cool.

Whip the egg whites until stiff and fold in the fish mixture with
a large metal spoon. Pour into 6 individual dishes, or into a 1-pint
(600 ml) soufflé dish, and leave to set overnight.

Leeks Vinaigrette
TIME 30 minutes   SERVES 4
CALORIES PER PORTION 130

This is a useful starter, as it can be served hot or cold, according to
the fluctuations in the weather.

8 small leeks	*8 small leeks*
1 chicken stock cube	*1 chicken stock cube*
salt and black pepper	*salt and black pepper*
1 small clove garlic	*1 small clove garlic*
2 tablespoons wine vinegar	*2 tablespoons wine vinegar*
1 teaspoon French mustard	*1 teaspoon French mustard*
8 tablespoons olive oil	*8 tablespoons olive oil*
2 dessertspoons chopped parsley	*2 dessertspoons chopped parsley*
2 dessertspoons chopped chives	*2 dessertspoons chopped chives*
1 teaspoon chopped capers	*1 teaspoon chopped capers*

Boil ½ pint (300 ml) water in a kettle. Trim the leeks, slit lengthways and wash under running water. Place in a pan large enough to

hold the leeks side by side. Dissolve the stock cube in the boiling
water and add to the pan. The liquid should come half way up the
leeks. Add a small pinch of salt. Cover and simmer gently for 8–10
minutes until just tender.

Meanwhile, crush the garlic with a little salt and place in a screw
top jar with the vinegar, mustard and olive oil. Shake until blended.
Chop the parsley, chives and capers and add to the dressing, with
more salt and pepper to taste.

Drain the leeks and pour the dressing over. Serve immediately,
or allow to marinate in the dressing overnight.

Marinaded Mushrooms
TIME 20 minutes, plus chilling   SERVES 4
CALORIES PER PORTION 87

1 lb button mushrooms	*500 g button mushrooms*
½ pint white wine	*300 ml white wine*
salt	*salt*
2 teaspoons lemon juice	*2 teaspoons lemon juice*
3 tablespoons corn oil	*3 tablespoons corn oil*
1 clove garlic	*1 clove garlic*
pepper	*pepper*
paprika	*paprika*
1 tablespoon chopped parsley	*1 tablespoon chopped parsley*

Wash or wipe the mushrooms. Do not peel. Place in a saucepan
with the wine and salt, squeeze the lemon juice and add, and simmer
for 5 minutes. Strain off the liquid into a jug. Place 2 tablespoons
of this liquid in a screw top jar and add 3 tablespoons oil. Crush
the garlic with a little salt and add to the jar with pepper and
paprika to taste. Shake well and pour over the mushrooms. Chill
for at least half an hour, or overnight, and sprinkle with parsley
before serving as a starter or as a salad.

Mushroom Soufflés

TIME 30 minutes SERVES 4
CALORIES PER PORTION 150

1 oz butter	*30 g butter*
1 small onion (2 oz)	*1 small onion (60 g)*
6 oz mushrooms	*175 g mushrooms*
8 oz cottage cheese	*250 g cottage cheese*
1 oz fresh white breadcrumbs	*30 g fresh white breadcrumbs*
1 tablespoon chopped parsley	*1 tablespoon chopped parsley*
salt and black pepper	*salt and black pepper*
1 egg white	*1 egg white*

Heat the oven to Gas 6; 400° F; 200° C.

Melt the butter in a frying pan and chop the onion finely. Fry for 3 minutes without browning. Meanwhile, wipe and chop the mushrooms. Add to the onions and cook for 2 minutes.

Sieve the cottage cheese into a bowl and grate in the breadcrumbs. Stir in the mushroom mixture. Chop the parsley and add with salt and pepper to taste. Grease 4 ramekins.

Whisk the egg white until stiff and fold gently into the mixture. Spoon into the ramekins, place on a baking tray and cook towards the top of the oven for 10 minutes until risen and golden. Serve immediately.

Pepper Salad

TIME 30 minutes SERVES 4 [F]
CALORIES PER PORTION 77

½ oz butter	*15 g butter*
1 dessertspoon corn oil	*1 dessertspoon corn oil*
2 medium onions (each 4 oz)	*2 medium onions (each 125 g)*
1 large green pepper	*1 large green pepper*
2 large red peppers	*2 large red peppers*
4 tomatoes	*4 tomatoes*

1 clove garlic   *1 clove garlic*
salt and black pepper   *salt and black pepper*

Boil 1 pint (600 ml) of water in a kettle. Heat the butter and oil in
a large sauté pan. Slice the onions and fry gently without browning
for 3 minutes. De-seed the peppers and cut into thin strips 2 inches
(5 cm) long. Add to the pan, mix well and cook for 5 minutes.

   Meanwhile, place the tomatoes in a bowl and cover with boiling
water. Skin and chop roughly. Crush the garlic with a little salt
and add to the pan with the tomatoes. Add salt and pepper to taste.
Simmer gently for 15 minutes, adjust the seasoning and serve hot or
cold.

Baked Eggs with Mushrooms
TIME 30 minutes   SERVES 4
CALORIES PER PORTION 189

4 oz mushrooms   *125 g mushrooms*
1 oz butter   *30 g butter*
1 spring onion   *1 spring onion*
salt and black pepper   *salt and black pepper*
4 eggs   *4 eggs*
4 tablespoons single cream   *4 tablespoons single cream*

Heat the oven to Gas 5; 375° F; 190° C.
   Boil 1 pint (600 ml) of water in a kettle. Wipe and slice the mushrooms. Melt the butter in a frying pan and chop the spring onion.
Add the mushrooms and onion to the pan and fry gently for 3
minutes. Remove from the heat, add salt and pepper to taste and
divide the mixture between four small ramekins.
   Break an egg into each dish, sprinkle with salt and pepper and
top each with 1 tablespoon of cream. Place the dishes in a roasting
tin and pour in the boiling water to within about ½ inch (1 cm) of
the rims. Place at the top of the oven and bake for 15 minutes or
until the whites are set and the yolks still runny.

Piperade
TIME 20 minutes   SERVES 2
CALORIES PER PORTION 268

The authentic Basque piperade includes ham, but for slimmers just use the vegetables.

¼ oz butter	*10 g butter*
1 medium onion (4 oz)	*1 medium onion (125 g)*
2 green peppers	*2 green peppers*
2 large tomatoes	*2 large tomatoes*
1 clove garlic	*1 clove garlic*
4 eggs	*4 eggs*
salt and pepper	*salt and pepper*

Boil enough water to cover the tomatoes. Heat the butter in an 8-inch (20-cm) frying pan. Slice the onion thinly and fry gently for 3 minutes. De-seed the peppers and cut into thin strips about 2 inches (5 cm) long. Add to the pan and cook for a further 5 minutes.

Place the tomatoes in a bowl and cover with boiling water. Crush the garlic. Skin and chop the tomatoes roughly and add to the pan with the garlic. Simmer the mixture until most of the juice from the tomatoes has evaporated. Beat the eggs with salt and pepper to taste and add to the mixture. Stir until the eggs are just set and serve immediately.

Cottage Cheese Omelette
TIME 15 minutes   SERVES 2
CALORIES PER PORTION 284

6 oz cottage cheese	*175 g cottage cheese*
3 eggs	*3 eggs*
1 tablespoon grated onion	*1 tablespoon grated onion*
1 tablespoon chopped chives	*1 tablespoon chopped chives*
salt and pepper	*salt and pepper*
¼ oz butter	*10 g butter*

Rub the cottage cheese through a sieve into a bowl. Separate the eggs and add the yolks to the cheese. Beat well. Grate the onion and chop the chives and add both to the cheese with salt and pepper to taste.

Heat the butter in a non-stick 8-inch (20-cm) frying pan and heat the grill. Meanwhile, whisk the egg whites until stiff and fold into the cheese mixture with a large metal spoon. Pour into the hot butter, turn the heat down and cook gently for 5–8 minutes, until the underside is golden brown. Place the pan under a medium grill and cook until the top is risen and golden – another 4 or 5 minutes. Serve immediately.

Sweet and Sour Cod Steaks

TIME 10 minutes   SERVES 2
CALORIES PER PORTION 237

This is rather more sour than sweet, and so terribly good for the slimmer's conscience.

2 cod steaks	*2 cod steaks*
corn oil	*corn oil*
1 tablespoon wine vinegar	*1 tablespoon wine vinegar*
1 tablespoon sherry	*1 tablespoon sherry*
1 tablespoon soya sauce	*1 tablespoon soya sauce*
1 orange	*1 orange*
1 pinch of ground ginger	*1 pinch of ground ginger*
8 oz can pineapple pieces	*250 g can pineapple pieces*
1 green pepper	*1 green pepper*

Heat the grill. Brush the cod steaks with oil and grill the fish for 5 minutes on each side, or until cooked through.

Meanwhile, place the vinegar, sherry and soya sauce in a small saucepan and heat to simmering point. Squeeze the orange juice and add to the pan with the ginger and pineapple, with its syrup. De-seed and chop the pepper and add to the pan. Simmer gently for 5 minutes, and pour over the fish.

Fish with Fennel

TIME 30 minutes   SERVES 4
CALORIES PER PORTION 218

1 oz butter	30 g butter
1 large onion (8 oz)	1 large onion (250 g)
1 large bulb fennel	1 large bulb fennel
4 cod steaks	4 cod steaks
salt and pepper	salt and pepper
¼ pint dry cider	150 ml dry cider
1 tablespoon Pernod (if available)	1 tablespoon Pernod (if available)

Heat the butter in a lidded sauté pan. Slice the onion finely and cook in the butter for 3 minutes without browning. Meanwhile, trim and thinly slice the fennel. Add to the pan and cook for a further 5 minutes.

Sprinkle the fish with a little salt and pepper and add to the pan with the cider and Pernod, if used. Cover the pan and simmer gently for 12–15 minutes until the fish is cooked through. Turn once during the cooking and add more salt and pepper if required.

Fish and Bacon Kebabs

TIME 25 minutes   SERVES 2
CALORIES PER PORTION 213

8 oz cod steak	250 g cod steak
½ lemon	½ lemon
salt and black pepper	salt and black pepper
5 rashers smoked streaky bacon	5 rashers smoked streaky bacon
2 tomatoes	2 tomatoes
8 button mushrooms	8 button mushrooms
corn oil	corn oil

Heat the grill. Cut the cod into 10 equal-sized pieces, squeeze the lemon juice over and sprinkle with salt and pepper. Halve the bacon rashers, quarter the tomatoes, wipe the mushrooms and remove the stalks.

Wrap a piece of fish in a half rasher of bacon and thread onto a skewer. Follow with a quarter of tomato and a whole mushroom. Repeat until both skewers are filled. Brush with oil and grill for 10 minutes, turning occasionally, until the bacon is crisp.

Smoked Fish Florentine
TIME 25 minutes   SERVES 4
CALORIES PER PORTION 302

1 lb smoked haddock	500 g smoked haddock
salt and black pepper	salt and black pepper
12 oz frozen leaf spinach	350 g frozen leaf spinach
2 oz Cheddar cheese	60 g Cheddar cheese
½ lemon	½ lemon
1 oz margarine	30 g margarine
1 oz flour	30 g flour
½ pint skimmed milk	300 ml skimmed milk
nutmeg	nutmeg

Place the fish and a pinch of salt in a saucepan with just enough water to cover. Bring to the boil and simmer gently for 8–10 minutes. Meanwhile heat the spinach in another saucepan. Grate the cheese, squeeze the lemon and heat the grill.

Melt the fat in a third pan, sprinkle in the flour and stir over a medium heat for 1 minute. Add the milk gradually, stirring constantly until thickened. Remove from the heat and stir in half the grated cheese.

Drain the spinach and mix with the lemon juice. Add grated nutmeg and black pepper to taste and place in a 1½-pint (900-ml) heatproof dish. Drain the fish, remove the skin and flake on top of the spinach. Pour the sauce over and sprinkle with the remaining cheese. Place under a hot grill until the cheese is melted and golden brown.

Fish Casserole

TIME 25 minutes   SERVES 2
CALORIES PER PORTION 238

1 large onion (8 oz)	*1 large onion (250 g)*
½ oz butter	*15 g butter*
2 tomatoes	*2 tomatoes*
small clove garlic	*small clove garlic*
2 steaks of cod or coley	*2 steaks of cod or coley*
(each 6 oz)	*(each 175 g)*
½ a bay leaf	*½ a bay leaf*
two sprigs parsley	*two sprigs parsley*
¼ pint dry cider or white wine	*150 ml dry cider or white wine*
salt and pepper	*salt and pepper*

Boil a kettle of water, enough to cover the tomatoes. Melt the butter in a saucepan large enough to hold the fish steaks. Chop the onion finely and fry gently in the butter for 3 minutes. Meanwhile, place the tomatoes in a bowl, cover with boiling water, skin and chop roughly. Add to the onions with the crushed garlic and cook for a further 5 minutes. Add the fish steaks, bay leaf, parsley and cider or wine. Season to taste and simmer gently for 12–15 minutes, depending on the thickness of the fish.

Plaice with Grapefruit

TIME 15 minutes   SERVES 4
CALORIES PER PORTION 292

4 small whole plaice	*4 small whole plaice*
1½ oz butter or margarine	*40 g butter or margarine*
salt	*salt*
1 grapefruit	*1 grapefruit*
1 oz flour	*25 g flour*
¼ pint skimmed milk	*150 ml skimmed milk*
4 oz peeled prawns	*125 g peeled prawns*

Dot the fish with ½ oz (15 g) butter or margarine, sprinkle with salt and grill for 5 minutes on each side. Meanwhile, grate half a teaspoon of grapefruit peel and squeeze the juice. Make up to ¼ pint (150 ml) if necessary with water.

Melt the remaining butter in a small saucepan, sprinkle in the flour and stir over a medium heat for 1 minute. Gradually add the milk and the grapefruit juice, stirring until thickened and smooth. Fold in the peel and the prawns and pour over the fish.

Hot Crab

TIME 30 minutes   SERVES 2
CALORIES PER PORTION 323

If you have a local fishmonger, you can buy prepared crabs and use the shells to serve the dish. Otherwise use crabmeat and serve in individual ovenproof dishes, or scallop shells.

1 oz butter	30 g butter
2 tablespoons chopped onion	2 tablespoons chopped onion
2 oz white breadcrumbs	60 g white breadcrumbs
2 small cooked crabs or	2 small cooked crabs or
4 oz crabmeat	125 g crabmeat
lemon juice	lemon juice
pepper and salt	pepper and salt
Worcestershire sauce	Worcestershire sauce
1 oz Cheddar cheese	30 g Cheddar cheese

Heat the butter in a frying pan. Chop the onion finely and fry for 3 minutes. Grate the breadcrumbs, add to the pan, and fry for a further 2 or 3 minutes or until browned. Add the crabmeat with lemon juice, pepper and Worcestershire sauce to taste. Add salt if necessary.

Heat the grill. Grate the cheese. Divide the crab mixture between the two crab shells, sprinkle with the cheese and grill until the cheese is golden.

Chicken with Red Peppers

TIME 30 minutes   SERVES 4
CALORIES PER PORTION 264

The sweetness of the red peppers blends well with the tomatoes in this dish. You can use green peppers, but the flavour is much sharper.

2 tablespoons corn oil	2 tablespoons corn oil
4 chicken joints	4 chicken joints
2 medium onions (each 4 oz)	2 medium onions (each 125 g)
2 red peppers	2 red peppers
1 lb tomatoes	500 g tomatoes
1 large clove garlic	1 large clove garlic
salt and black pepper	salt and black pepper

Boil enough water in a kettle to cover the tomatoes. Heat 1 tablespoon of oil in a deep sauté pan and brown the chicken joints on both sides. Reduce the heat and cook gently while preparing the vegetables.

Heat the remaining oil in a saucepan. Slice the onions and fry gently for 3 minutes. De-seed and slice the peppers and add to the onions. Mix well and continue to cook.

Pour boiling water over the tomatoes, skin and chop roughly. Crush the garlic with a little salt and add to the vegetables with the tomatoes. Season to taste with salt and black pepper. Cover and simmer gently until the tomatoes are soft.

Check the seasoning, pour the vegetable mixture over the chicken joints and continue to simmer until the chicken is cooked through.

Sweet and Sour Chicken with Beansprouts

TIME 30 minutes   SERVES 4
CALORIES PER PORTION 290

Beansprouts make a good alternative to rice as a base for slimmers' dishes. You can, of course, use rice instead for non-weight-worriers.

4 chicken joints	*4 chicken joints*
corn oil	*corn oil*
salt and pepper	*salt and pepper*
1 level tablespoon cornflour	*1 level tablespoon cornflour*
¼ pint chicken stock or 1 chicken stock cube	*150 ml chicken stock or 1 chicken stock cube*
3 tablespoons vinegar	*3 tablespoons vinegar*
1 tablespoon tomato ketchup	*1 tablespoon tomato ketchup*
2 teaspoons soya sauce	*2 teaspoons soya sauce*
3 teaspoons Worcestershire sauce	*3 teaspoons Worcestershire sauce*
1 medium onion (4 oz)	*1 medium onion (125 g)*
7 oz can pineapple chunks	*200 g can pineapple chunks*
8 oz beansprouts	*250 g beansprouts*

If using a stock cube, boil ¼ pint (150 ml) of water in a kettle. Heat the grill, brush the chicken joints with a little oil and sprinkle with salt and pepper. Cook under a medium heat for 10–12 minutes each side.

Meanwhile, place the cornflour in a cup and mix to a smooth cream with a tablespoon of water. Place the chicken stock in a small saucepan, or crumble in the stock cube and add the boiling water. Add the vinegar, ketchup, soya sauce and Worcestershire sauce. Grate in the onion.

Drain ¼ pint (150 ml) of juice from the pineapple and add to the mixture. Stir in the cornflour and bring to the boil, stirring. Chop two slices of pineapple and stir in. Allow to simmer gently.

When the chicken is cooked, heat 1 teaspoon of oil in a large saucepan, add the beansprouts and cook quickly, stirring gently, for 2 minutes. Sprinkle with a little salt if required. Place the chicken joints in a serving dish, pour the sauce over and serve the beansprouts separately.

Kidneys and Tomatoes in Wine
TIME 25 minutes   SERVES 4
CALORIES PER PORTION 220

12 oz lamb's kidneys	*350 g lamb's kidneys*
1 oz butter	*30 g butter*
1 large onion (6 oz)	*1 large onion (175 g)*
2 level tablespoons flour	*2 level tablespoons flour*
½ pint beef stock or 1 beef stock cube	*300 ml beef stock or 1 beef stock cube*
8 oz tomatoes	*250 g tomatoes*
4 tablespoons wine	*4 tablespoons wine*
thyme	*thyme*
salt and pepper	*salt and pepper*

Boil 1½ pints (900 ml) water in a kettle and warm a plate. Meanwhile, halve and core the kidneys and cut into small pieces. Melt the butter in a saucepan and sauté the kidneys quickly for 2 minutes. Remove from the pan to the warm plate. Chop the onion and fry in the same pan for 3 minutes. Sprinkle in the flour and stir over a medium heat for 1 minute. Add the stock or crumble in the stock cube and add ½ pint (300 ml) of boiling water. Simmer, stirring, until smooth and thick.

Place the tomatoes in a bowl and cover with boiling water. Skin and chop roughly. Add to the pan with the wine and a pinch of thyme. Season to taste and simmer for 10 minutes. Return the kidneys and any juices to the pan and heat through for 1 minute.

Liver with Rosemary
TIME 15 minutes   SERVES 2
CALORIES PER PORTION 364

1 oz butter	*30 g butter*
1 tablespoon corn oil	*1 tablespoon corn oil*
2 medium onions (each 4 oz)	*2 medium onions (each 125 g)*

4 sprigs fresh rosemary	*4 sprigs fresh rosemary*
8 oz lamb's liver	*250 g lamb's liver*
1 tablespoon flour	*1 tablespoon flour*
salt and pepper	*salt and pepper*
2 tablespoons red wine	*2 tablespoons red wine*
2 tablespoons chicken stock or	*2 tablespoons chicken stock or*
1 stock cube	*1 stock cube*

Boil ½ pint (300 ml) water to dissolve the stock cube. Heat the butter and oil in a large frying pan. Slice the onions, gently fry with the rosemary sprigs for 5 minutes. Meanwhile, cut the liver into 1-inch (2-cm) strips and toss in the flour mixed with a little salt and pepper. Remove the rosemary sprigs from the pan, turn up the heat and add the liver. Sauté for 1–2 minutes, stirring to cook all sides. Do not overcook. Add the red wine and chicken stock, or dissolve the stock cube in the boiling water and use 2 tablespoons of this stock, and simmer for another minute or two.

Beefburgers
TIME 20 minutes   SERVES 4
CALORIES PER PORTION 226

This method of making beefburgers was given to me by an American friend who developed a talent for making mince taste like real food when he was an impecunious student. The addition of iced water makes the burgers lighter. If you have a processor, always buy lean chuck or blade steak, remove any fat, and grind the meat yourself, rather than buying butchers' mince, which is always fattier.

1 lb minced lean beef	*500 g minced lean beef*
1 medium onion (4 oz)	*1 medium onion (125 g)*
1 egg yolk	*1 egg yolk*
pinch mixed herbs	*pinch mixed herbs*
salt and pepper	*salt and pepper*
Worcestershire sauce	*Worcestershire sauce*
oil for frying	*oil for frying*

Place an ice cube in a tablespoon of water in a glass. Place the minced beef in a bowl and grate the onion into it. Add the egg yolk, with a pinch of mixed herbs and salt, pepper and Worcestershire sauce to taste and mix well. Heat a very little oil in a frying pan.

Add a tablespoon of iced water to the mince and mix well with a fork. Form into four burgers, 1 inch (2 cm) thick, and fry for about 5 minutes on each side, or less if liked rare.

Fennel with Bacon
TIME 30 minutes   SERVES 4
CALORIES PER PORTION 132

This makes a good accompaniment to low-calorie, grilled fish. Or serve it for 2 people on its own as a supper dish (don't forget to double the calories).

4 oz streaky bacon	125 g streaky bacon
2 medium onions (each 4 oz)	2 medium onions (each 125 g)
2 large bulbs fennel	2 large bulbs fennel
6 tomatoes	6 tomatoes
salt and black pepper	salt and black pepper

Boil 1 pint (600 ml) water in a kettle. De-rind the bacon and fry over a medium heat until crisp. Meanwhile, slice the onions. Remove the bacon from the pan and fry the onions in the bacon fat. Separate the fennel layers and wash away any grit. Cut into strips and add to the onion. Continue to cook while preparing the tomatoes.

Place the tomatoes in a bowl and cover with boiling water. Skin, chop roughly and add to the pan. Add salt and pepper to taste, mix well, and simmer gently for 10 minutes, or until the tomatoes are soft. Chop the bacon, and stir into the vegetable mixture.

Alaskan Omelette
TIME 10 minutes   SERVES 1
CALORIES PER PORTION 240

butter	*butter*
2 large eggs	*2 large eggs*
vanilla essence	*vanilla essence*
liquid sweetener	*liquid sweetener*
1 oz slice vanilla ice cream	*30 g slice vanilla ice cream*

Heat a knob of butter the size of a hazelnut in a small omelette pan, and at the same time heat the grill. Separate the eggs and whisk the whites until stiff. Add one yolk with a few drops of vanilla essence and sweetener to taste, and whisk again.

Pour into the pan and cook over a gentle heat for about 3 minutes, until golden underneath. Place the pan under the grill until the top of the omelette is golden. Slide onto a warm plate, place the ice cream on one half and fold the other over. Serve immediately.

Apple Snow
TIME 30 minutes   SERVES 3
CALORIES PER PORTION 140

Don't try to cut down the calories by using liquid sweetener here. The flavour of the apples is too delicate to mask any synthetic taste.

1 lb Bramley apples	*500 g Bramley apples*
1–2 oz sugar	*25–50 g sugar*
2 teaspoons lemon juice	*2 teaspoons lemon juice*
2 egg whites	*2 egg whites*

Peel, core and slice the apples and place in a saucepan with 2 table-spoons of water and up to 2 oz (50 g) sugar to taste. Simmer for 8–10 minutes until pulpy. Drain off any excess liquid and rub the fruit through a sieve. Spread on a plate and place in the fridge to cool quickly.

Whisk the egg whites until stiff. Fold in the apple pulp and spoon into 3 individual glasses.

Hot Grapefruit Soufflé

TIME 30 minutes   SERVES 2
CALORIES PER PORTION 160

1 large grapefruit	1 large grapefruit
2 large eggs	2 large eggs
3 level tablespoons icing sugar	3 level tablespoons icing sugar

Preheat the oven to Gas 5; 375° F; 190° C.

Grate the rind of the grapefruit. Cut the fruit into two and squeeze the juice of one half. Remove the segments from the other half, discarding the pith, pips and skin. Separate the eggs. Beat the egg yolks in a bowl with the icing sugar until thick and light. In another bowl whisk the whites until stiff.

Stir the grapefruit rind into the yolks with 1 teaspoon of the juice and fold into the whites with a large metal spoon, turning over gently until mixed.

Place the segments in a 1-pint (600-ml) soufflé dish, spoon the mixture over and bake for 15 minutes until risen and golden. Serve immediately.

Pears with Strawberry Sauce

TIME 10 minutes   SERVES 2
CALORIES PER PORTION 188

4 oz strawberries	125 g strawberries
1 teaspoon cornflour	1 teaspoon cornflour
liquid sweetener	liquid sweetener
2 oz cream cheese	60 g cream cheese
1 tablespoon natural yogurt	1 tablespoon natural yogurt
1 large ripe pear	1 large ripe pear

Sieve the strawberries into a small pan. Mix the cornflour with a little water to make a thin cream, pour into the strawberry purée and heat through. Add sweetener to taste.

Beat the cream cheese with the yogurt. Peel, halve and core the pear and fill the hollows with the cream cheese mixture. Pour the strawberry sauce over and serve immediately.

Orange Cheesecake
TIME 10 minutes plus setting   SERVES 6
CALORIES PER PORTION 115

½ can concentrated orange juice, thawed	*½ can concentrated orange juice, thawed*
½ oz sachet gelatine	*15 g sachet gelatine*
8 oz cottage cheese	*250 g cottage cheese*
5 fl oz natural low fat yogurt	*150 ml natural low fat yogurt*
2 egg whites	*2 egg whites*
3 oranges	*3 oranges*
liquid sweetener	*liquid sweetener*

Simmer a little water in a small pan. Place a bowl on top containing the concentrated orange juice. Sprinkle on the gelatine and stir until dissolved. Remove from the heat. Sieve the cottage cheese and mix with the yogurt. Add the gelatine mixture.

Whisk the egg whites stiffly, and peel and segment one orange. Fold segments and egg whites into the cheese mixture. Sweeten to taste with liquid sweetener. Spoon into a loose-bottomed 7-inch (18-cm) flan tin and allow to set overnight or for at least 30 minutes. Peel the remaining oranges, divide into segments and arrange on top of the cheesecake.

Orange Cream
TIME 10 minutes plus setting   SERVES 4
CALORIES PER PORTION 105

½ oz sachet gelatine
5 oz natural low fat yogurt
1 can concentrated orange
  juice, thawed
liquid sweetener
1 orange

15 g sachet gelatine
150 ml natural low fat yogurt
1 can concentrated orange
  juice, thawed
liquid sweetener
1 orange

Place 2 tablespoons of water in a small bowl and set over a pan of simmering water. Sprinkle in the gelatine and stir until dissolved. Remove from the heat.

Place the yogurt in a bowl and whisk in the concentrated orange juice. Stir ½ pint (300 ml) of cold water into the gelatine and whisk into the orange mixture. Add liquid sweetener to taste and pour into 4 individual glasses. Leave to set for 1 hour or overnight. Decorate with orange segments.

LOW-CHOLESTEROL

Health foods are one thing. Foods for health quite another. There is absolutely no need to buy cranky and usually expensive 'special foods' – and in any case it is as well to remember that there are fashions in food and medicine just as in clothes and furniture. The world happens to be on a bulk-is-beautiful, fat-is-fearsome kick at the moment, but it wasn't so long ago that we were being urged to cut down bread and potatoes and eat lots of eggs, meat and milk. And how do those nutritionists who preach that you must start the day with a cooked breakfast account for the fact that generations of the rest of Europe have gone to work on a croissant?

However, the Royal College of Physicians did publish its conviction that a cholesterol-lowering diet would help minimize the risk of coronary heart disease – one of the major killers in our stressful, under-exercised, over-indulged Western world. The subject of low-cholesterol cookery is big enough for an entire book, but often people don't bother with such specialized cookery until it is too late – until someone in the family actually has, or is threatened with, a heart condition.

So this chapter is simply an introduction to the principles, which you can easily apply to your normal everyday cooking, without feeling you are being faddy, but with the knowledge that you can't be doing yourself any harm and may be doing yourself a lot of good. Obviously, if you have reason to be really worried about your heart or health, you should see a doctor, but if you simply want to make sure you don't take in too many fatty substances, these are the main points to remember:

Cholesterol is a normal constituent of all animal tissue. Foods rich in it are egg yolks, liver, kidneys, dairy produce. Fruit, vegetables and vegetable fats contain none. Therefore, a simple cholesterol-reducing diet cuts down on meats and dairy foods and steps up the vegetable and fibre content.

There are three sorts of fat:

1. Saturated fats which tend to raise the cholesterol. These are butter, hard cheeses, lard, suet. Even when it isn't actually bordered by layers of fat, lean meat contains a high proportion of saturated fat, which is why you should keep portions of beef, lamb and pork to small servings.

2. Mono-unsaturated fats are those which do not contain cholesterol, but don't have any positive cholesterol-lowering effect. These include olive oil and peanut oil.

3. Polyunsaturated fats are those that actually help to keep the cholesterol level down. These are all vegetable based – corn oil, sunflower oil and soya bean oil, and margarines which specifically say they are polyunsaturated. Be careful. Some margarines, which really do taste very much like butter and often have a percentage of butter in them, say they are lower in saturated fats. This does not necessarily mean they are positively polyunsaturated.

If your aim is to keep cholesterol down, but you are not concerned about losing weight, consider the following lists:

Unrestricted foods: Wholemeal bread, breakfast cereals, rice, pasta, polyunsaturated margarine, vegetable oils, skimmed milk, low fat cottage cheese and yogurt, egg white, clear soups or those made with skimmed milk, all green, root and pulse vegetables, all fruits, pastries and biscuits made with polyunsaturated fat or egg white, tea, coffee, fruit squashes, minerals, nuts (except coconut and cashew nuts).

Restricted foods: Beef, lamb, ham or pork in 2 oz portions, chicken, turkey or veal in 3 oz portions, fish in 4–6 oz portions. Two eggs per week. Marmalade, jam and honey in moderation.

Forbidden foods: Milk, including sterilized, evaporated, condensed and powdered full-cream milk, cream, cream substitute, soured cream, butter, cheese, ordinary margarine, lard, dripping, suet, meat fat, coconut and palm oil, fat minced meat, sausages, luncheon meats, corned beef, heart, liver, kidney, brains, sweetbreads, canned meats, goose, duck, game, shellfish, fish roe, baked beans, potato crisps, egg noodles, bought cakes and biscuits, puddings prepared with forbidden fats or egg yolk, ice cream, mayonnaise, salad cream, chocolate, malted milks, coconut, cashew nuts.

Remember that cholesterol control is not the same thing as weight control. Some fanatics will tell you that you can eat as much whole-wheat pasta and bread as you like and you will lose weight. It isn't true in all cases. If you tend to put on weight, you must count calories, too, so all the recipes in this section show the calorie content to help you pick the least fattening, if you wish.

Beetroot Soup
TIME 30 minutes   SERVES 4
CALORIES PER PORTION 132

I wouldn't dignify this with the name of bortsch, which should be made with uncooked beetroot. But that takes too long, so this recipe is adapted for ready-cooked beetroot. You do need a blender or processor, though.

1½ pints chicken stock or 2 chicken stock cubes	900 ml chicken stock or 2 chicken stock cubes
1 oz polyunsaturated margarine	30 g polyunsaturated margarine
1 medium onion (6 oz)	1 medium onion (175 g)
1 medium potato (4 oz)	1 medium potato (125 g)
8 oz cooked beetroot	250 g cooked beetroot
salt and pepper	salt and pepper
4 tablespoons natural low fat yogurt	4 tablespoons natural low fat yogurt

Heat the stock in a saucepan or, if using cubes, boil 1½ pints (900 ml) of water in a kettle. Melt the margarine over a medium heat in a large saucepan. Chop the onion and cook gently while peeling and dicing the potato. Add to the onion. Peel and dice the beetroot and add.

Pour in the hot stock, or dissolve the cubes in the boiling water and add with salt to taste. Cover and simmer for 15–18 minutes, until the potato is tender.

Pour into a blender or processor and blend until smooth. Return to the pan, adjust the seasoning and heat through. Pour into bowls and place a tablespoon of yogurt in the centre of each just before serving.

Spinach Soup
TIME 20 minutes   SERVES 4   [F]
CALORIES PER PORTION 98

¾ pint chicken stock or 1 chicken stock cube	*450 ml chicken stock or 1 chicken stock cube*
1 oz polyunsaturated margarine	*30 g polyunsaturated margarine*
1 large onion (6 oz)	*1 large onion (175 g)*
8 oz frozen leaf spinach	*250 g frozen leaf spinach*
salt and black pepper	*salt and black pepper*
¼ pint skimmed milk, fresh or powdered	*150 ml skimmed milk, fresh or powdered*
nutmeg	*nutmeg*

Heat the chicken stock in a small pan or boil ¾ pint (450 ml) water in a kettle. Meanwhile melt the margarine in a large saucepan, chop the onion and fry gently for 3 minutes without browning. Add the spinach, still frozen, with the hot stock or the crumbled stock cube and water. Season with salt and black pepper and simmer gently for 10 minutes. Meanwhile make up the skimmed milk, if using powder.

Place the soup in a blender or processor and blend until smooth. Return to the pan, add the milk and adjust the seasoning, adding ground nutmeg to taste. Heat through without boiling.

Carrot Soup with Dill
TIME 30 minutes   SERVES 4   [F]
CALORIES PER PORTION 112

You need a blender or processor to purée the carrots. It can be done by hand – but not in the time.

1 pint chicken stock or
  1 chicken stock cube
	600 ml chicken stock or
	  1 chicken stock cube

1 lb carrots	500 g carrots
1 oz polyunsaturated margarine	30 g polyunsaturated margarine
1 medium onion (6 oz)	1 medium onion (175 g)

1 tablespoon chopped fresh
  dill or 1 teaspoon dried dill
	1 tablespoon chopped fresh
	  dill or 1 teaspoon dried dill

salt and black pepper	salt and black pepper
¼ pint skimmed milk	150 ml skimmed milk

Heat the chicken stock, or boil 1 pint (600 ml) of water in a kettle if using a stock cube. Peel and chop the carrots finely. Heat the margarine in a large saucepan and meanwhile chop the onion. Add to the pan and cook gently for 3 minutes.

Add the carrots and the hot stock, or crumble in the stock cube and add 1 pint (600 ml) of boiling water. Add the dill and salt to taste. Cover and simmer for 15 minutes until the carrots are soft. Place in a blender or processor and blend. Return to the pan, adjust the seasoning and add the milk, and heat through gently without boiling.

Aubergines with Tomato Sauce
TIME 25 minutes   SERVES 4
CALORIES PER PORTION 95

This dish makes an attractive hot accompaniment to chops or chicken, or it can be served cold as a starter. If you don't want to use the oven for the aubergines alone, you can fry them for about 5–8 minutes, but they absorb a lot more oil that way.

3 tablespoons corn oil	*3 tablespoons corn oil*
1 large onion (6 oz)	*1 large onion (175 g)*
1½ lbs tomatoes	*750 g tomatoes*
1 large clove garlic	*1 large clove garlic*
salt and black pepper	*salt and black pepper*
2–3 teaspoons sugar	*2–3 teaspoons sugar*
2 tablespoons chopped parsley	*2 tablespoons chopped parsley*
2 aubergines, each 8 oz	*2 aubergines, each 250 g*

Heat the oven to Gas 6; 400° F; 200° C.

Boil 2 pints (1.25 litres) of water in a kettle. Heat 1 tablespoon of oil in a large saucepan. Meanwhile chop the onion finely, add to the pan and fry gently for 2 minutes without browning. Place the tomatoes in a bowl and pour boiling water over. Skin, chop roughly and add to the pan. Crush the garlic with a little salt, and add to the pan with the sugar. Chop the parsley and stir in 1 tablespoon. Simmer gently, uncovered, until soft and thick. Adjust the seasoning to taste.

Meanwhile, wipe the aubergines and cut into ¼-inch (1-cm) slices. Sprinkle with salt on both sides and pat dry with a paper towel. Pour the remaining oil onto a plate and dip each slice on both sides. Grease a large roasting tin lightly with any remaining oil and place the aubergine slices in it in one layer. Bake for 10–15 minutes until tender. They should be golden but not brown underneath.

Turn the aubergines onto a plate, golden side up. Place a spoonful of tomato sauce on the centre of each, sprinkle with the remaining parsley, and serve hot or cold.

Hot Stuffed Tomatoes

TIME 30 minutes   SERVES 4   [F]
CALORIES PER PORTION 140

Prepared packets of breadcrumbs and parsley in the freezer are useful for this recipe.

1 tablespoon corn oil	*1 tablespoon corn oil*
½ oz polyunsaturated margarine	*15 g polyunsaturated margarine*
1 medium onion (4 oz)	*1 medium onion (125 g)*

6 large tomatoes	6 large tomatoes
4 oz fresh wholemeal breadcrumbs	125 g fresh wholemeal breadcrumbs
2 tablespoons chopped parsley	2 tablespoons chopped parsley
1 oz stuffed olives	25 g stuffed olives
salt and pepper	salt and pepper

Heat the oven to Gas 6; 400° F; 200° C.

Heat the oil and margarine in a saucepan. Chop the onion and fry gently for 5 minutes without browning. Meanwhile halve the tomatoes and scoop out the centres. Place the tomato cases on a baking tray. Add the tomato pulp to the onions with the breadcrumbs and parsley. Chop the olives finely and add, with salt and pepper to taste. Mix well and spoon into the tomato halves.

Place the tomatoes towards the top of the oven, and bake for 15–20 minutes until brown and crusty on top.

Mousseline of Mushrooms

TIME 15 minutes   SERVES 4
CALORIES PER PORTION 155

1 oz polyunsaturated margarine	30 g polyunsaturated margarine
1 small onion (2 oz)	1 small onion (60 g)
8 oz button mushrooms	250 g button mushrooms
1 teaspoon lemon juice	1 teaspoon lemon juice
5 fl oz natural low fat yogurt	150 ml natural low fat yogurt
salt	salt
nutmeg	nutmeg
cayenne pepper	cayenne pepper

Heat the margarine in a large saucepan. Chop the onion finely, and fry gently in the margarine for 3 minutes without browning. Meanwhile, wipe the mushrooms and slice, including all but the tough ends of the stalks. Add to the pan and cook with the onions for 2 minutes.

Strain off any juices and place in a blender or processor with the lemon juice. Purée until smooth. Add 1 tablespoon of yogurt and blend again. Add salt, and grated nutmeg to taste. Place in a sieve over a bowl and chill for 10 minutes to allow any extra liquid to drain away.

Spoon into 4 ramekins, place a tablespoon of yogurt on each and sprinkle with cayenne pepper. Serve with hot wholemeal toast.

Plaice with Horseradish

TIME 20 minutes   SERVES 4
CALORIES PER PORTION 202

You can use cod or haddock steaks for this dish, if you have no fishmonger to skin the plaice fillets – it's a nuisance doing it yourself.

4 small plaice, filleted and skinned	4 small plaice, filleted and skinned
1 small onion	1 small onion
salt	salt
1 bay leaf	1 bay leaf
1 dessertspoon cornflour	1 dessertspoon cornflour
10 fl oz natural low fat yogurt	300 ml natural low fat yogurt
1–2 teaspoons horseradish sauce	1–2 teaspoons horseradish sauce
1 tablespoon chopped parsley	1 tablespoon chopped parsley

Roll up each fillet of plaice and secure with a wooden cocktail stick. Lay the rolls in a pan large enough to accommodate them in one layer. Slice the onion and add with a pinch of salt and a bay leaf. Pour in just enough water to cover and simmer very gently for 8–10 minutes, or until the fish is cooked through.

Meanwhile, place the cornflour in a bowl and mix to a smooth thin cream with a little water. Stir in the yogurt. Turn into a small pan and bring to the boil. Cook for 2 minutes, stirring. Add the horseradish sauce to taste. Chop the parsley, stir into the sauce, and pour over the fish.

Stuffed Plaice
TIME 30 minutes　SERVES 2
CALORIES PER PORTION 500

It helps to have ready-prepared crumbs for this recipe.

2½ oz polyunsaturated margarine	75 g polyunsaturated margarine
4 oz mushrooms	120 g mushrooms
2 oz breadcrumbs	60 g breadcrumbs
rind of 1 lemon	rind of 1 lemon
salt and pepper	salt and pepper
2 plaice trimmed into four fillets and skinned	2 plaice trimmed into four fillets and skinned
1 oz flour	30 g flour
½ pint skimmed milk	300 ml skimmed milk

Heat the oven to Gas 6; 400° F; 200° C.

Heat 1 oz (30 g) margarine in a small pan. Wipe the mushrooms and chop finely. Place in a bowl with the breadcrumbs, and grate in the rind of the lemon. Season to taste and mix with the melted margarine. Divide the mixture between the four fillets of plaice and roll up. Place the fish rolls in an ovenproof dish, dot with ½ oz (15 g) margarine and bake for 15 minutes.

Meanwhile, melt the remaining margarine in the small pan, sprinkle in the flour and add the milk gradually, stirring constantly until smooth and thick. Season to taste and pour over the fish.

Baked Fish Steaks with Spinach
TIME 30 minutes　SERVES 2
CALORIES PER PORTION 233

If you think you don't like spinach, don't dismiss all dishes which include it. It can be very good with the addition of a little nutmeg or lemon.

8 oz frozen leaf spinach	*250 g frozen leaf spinach*
1 tablespoon corn oil	*1 tablespoon corn oil*
1 medium onion (4 oz)	*1 medium onion (125 g)*
4 tomatoes	*4 tomatoes*
1 tablespoon chopped parsley	*1 tablespoon chopped parsley*
1 teaspoon dried dill	*1 teaspoon dried dill*
1 clove garlic	*1 clove garlic*
salt and black pepper	*salt and black pepper*
knob polyunsaturated margarine	*knob polyunsaturated margarine*
2 cod or haddock steaks	*2 cod or haddock steaks*
lemon juice	*lemon juice*
2 tablespoons dry white wine	*2 tablespoons dry white wine*

Pre-heat oven to Gas 6; 400° F; 200° C.

Boil enough water to cover the tomatoes. Place the spinach in a pan with 2 tablespoons of water and heat slowly to defrost. Heat the oil in a sauté pan, chop the onion finely and cook over a medium heat while preparing the tomatoes. Place these in a bowl and pour boiling water over. Skin, chop roughly and add to the onions with the parsley and dill and the garlic crushed with a little salt. Add salt and pepper to taste.

Drain the spinach and mix with a knob of margarine and seasoning to taste. Spoon into a deep ovenproof dish and place the fish steaks on top. Sprinkle with salt and a squeeze of lemon juice and cover with the onion and tomato mixture. Add the wine and bake for 15 minutes.

Curried Vegetables with Rice
TIME 30 minutes   SERVES 4
CALORIES PER PORTION 557

12 oz long grain rice	*350 g long grain rice*
salt	*salt*
½ pint chicken stock or 1 chicken stock cube	*300 ml chicken stock or 1 chicken stock cube*

2 oz polyunsaturated margarine	*60 g polyunsaturated margarine*
2 potatoes	*2 potatoes*
1 cauliflower	*1 cauliflower*
1 large onion (8 oz)	*1 large onion (250 g)*
1 clove garlic	*1 clove garlic*
1 tablespoon curry paste or powder	*1 tablespoon curry paste or powder*
1 teaspoon cumin seeds	*1 teaspoon cumin seeds*
4 oz frozen whole green beans	*125 g frozen whole green beans*
6 oz frozen sweet corn	*175 g frozen sweet corn*
1 dessertspoon flour or cornflour	*1 dessertspoon flour or cornflour*

Bring 2 pints (1·25 litres) of water to the boil in a kettle. Measure 22 fl oz (650 ml) into a saucepan and add the rice with 1 teaspoon of salt. Cover and cook according to the quick method on page 75. Heat the chicken stock, or dissolve the stock cube in ½ pint (300 ml) boiling water.

Melt the margarine gently in a large saucepan. Meanwhile, peel the potatoes and cut into 1-inch (2-cm) dice. Divide the cauliflower into florets. Toss both in the margarine and cook gently, covered, while preparing the other vegetables.

Slice the onion and add to the pan. Crush the garlic with a little salt and add. Add the curry paste or powder with the cumin seeds, mix well and pour in the hot chicken stock. Add a good pinch of salt, bring to the boil and simmer, covered, for 8 minutes. Add the beans and sweet corn and simmer for a further 5 minutes, or until all the vegetables are just tender. Mix the flour or cornflour with a little water to make a smooth, thin paste and stir into the mixture. Cook, stirring, for 1 minute. Arrange the rice round the edge of a dish and spoon the vegetables into the centre.

Sesame Cabbage

TIME 20 minutes   SERVES 4
CALORIES PER PORTION 117

Toasted sesame seeds give a nutty flavour to vegetables or salad. You can use 1 teaspoon of caraway seeds in this dish if you prefer.

2 fl oz chicken stock, or ½ a chicken stock cube	60 ml chicken stock or ½ a chicken stock cube
1 oz polyunsaturated margarine	30 g polyunsaturated margarine
1 small onion (2 oz)	1 small onion (60 g)
1–1½ lbs white cabbage	500–750 g white cabbage
salt and black pepper	salt and black pepper
1 oz sesame seeds	25 g sesame seeds

Heat the chicken stock or boil ¼ pint (150 ml) water in a kettle. Heat the margarine in a large saucepan. Chop the onion finely and cook over a gentle heat without browning. Meanwhile, remove the outer leaves and stalks from the cabbage and shred finely.

Add the cabbage to the saucepan with a pinch of salt and pour in the stock, or dissolve the stock cube in ¼ pint (150 ml) boiling water and use 2 fl oz (60 ml) for the cabbage. Cover and simmer for 5–8 minutes, or until just tender.

Meanwhile, place the sesame seeds on a heatproof plate and place under a hot grill until golden. They will start jumping about when they get hot, so keep watch. Drain the cabbage, season with black pepper and more salt if necessary, and stir in the sesame seeds.

Red Cabbage and Apple

TIME 30 minutes   SERVES 4   [F]
CALORIES PER PORTION 175

Usually red cabbage benefits from long, slow cooking – at least an hour. But this quick version is tasty and takes only 10 minutes to prepare, 20 minutes to cook, which leaves enough time for the preparation of another course.

1 oz polyunsaturated margarine	*30 g polyunsaturated margarine*
1 large onion (6 oz)	*1 large onion (175 g)*
1½ lbs red cabbage	*750 g red cabbage*
salt and black pepper	*salt and black pepper*
2 tablespoons sugar	*2 tablespoons sugar*
4 tablespoons wine vinegar	*4 tablespoons wine vinegar*
2 Cox's apples	*2 Cox's apples*
nutmeg	*nutmeg*

Heat the margarine in a saucepan. Meanwhile slice the onion, add to the pan and cook gently for 3 minutes without browning. Remove the hard core of the cabbage and chop finely (shred first, then chop the shreds). Add to the pan with half a teaspoon of salt, the sugar, vinegar and two tablespoons of water. Peel, core and slice the apples and add. Cover and simmer for 15–20 minutes, until tender. If any liquid remains, raise the heat and boil until evaporated. Adjust the seasoning and add grated nutmeg to taste.

Caraway Potato Salad

TIME 30 minutes   SERVES 4
CALORIES PER PORTION 173

1½ lbs new potatoes	*750 g new potatoes*
salt and pepper	*salt and pepper*
2 tablespoons chopped onion	*2 tablespoons chopped onion*
2 tablespoons caraway seeds	*2 tablespoons caraway seeds*
8 fl oz natural low fat yogurt	*¼ litre natural low fat yogurt*

Put enough water to cover the potatoes in a saucepan and bring to the boil. Meanwhile scrub the potatoes, do not peel. Add to the pan with a pinch of salt, cover and boil for 15–20 minutes until tender.

Meanwhile, chop the onion and place in a large bowl with the caraway seeds and yogurt. Drain the potatoes, cut into dice and add to the yogurt mixture while still warm. Toss well, adjust the seasoning and serve warm, or chill until required.

Three Bean Salad
TIME 25 minutes   SERVES 4
CALORIES PER PORTION 310

This is one of the few recipes in this book where canned food is the main ingredient. The reason is that beans play a major part in low-cholesterol diets, but unless you have a pressure cooker they take ages to prepare from scratch.

15 oz can red kidney beans	430 g can red kidney beans
15 oz can butter beans	430 g can butter beans
15 oz can cannellini beans	430 g can cannellini beans
1 clove garlic	1 clove garlic
1 stick celery	1 stick celery
1 red pepper	1 red pepper
1 green pepper	1 green pepper
1 dessertspoon chopped parsley	1 dessertspoon chopped parsley
2 spring onions	2 spring onions
salt and black pepper	salt and black pepper
2 teaspoons wine vinegar	2 teaspoons wine vinegar
7 teaspoons corn oil	7 teaspoons corn oil
½ teaspoon made mustard	½ teaspoon made mustard
thyme	thyme
1 teaspoon lemon juice	1 teaspoon lemon juice

Place the red beans in a sieve, wash under cold water and drain. Place in a bowl. Repeat with the other beans, keeping each type separate. Crush the garlic, chop the celery finely, de-seed and cut the red pepper into $\frac{1}{2}$-inch (1-cm) squares and the green pepper into small dice. Chop the parsley and the spring onions.

In each of three teacups place half a teaspoon of salt and a little black pepper. To the first, add 1 teaspoon vinegar, the garlic and 3 teaspoons corn oil. Add to the kidney beans with the celery and mix well.

To the second cup add the mustard, a pinch of thyme, 1 teaspoon vinegar and 2 teaspoons corn oil. Add to the butter beans with the red pepper and spring onions. To the third cup add 1 teaspoon lemon juice, 2 teaspoons corn oil, and the parsley. Add to the cannellini beans and mix well. Adjust the seasoning of each salad to taste.

Arrange the red beans across the centre of a large flat dish or meat plate, with the butter beans on one side and the cannellini on the other.

Chicken in Paprika Sauce

TIME 25 minutes   SERVES 2
CALORIES PER PORTION 380

2 chicken joints	*2 chicken joints*
corn oil	*corn oil*
1 oz polyunsaturated margarine	*30 g polyunsaturated margarine*
1 medium onion (4 oz)	*1 medium onion (125 g)*
1 small clove garlic (optional)	*1 small clove garlic (optional)*
salt and black pepper	*salt and black pepper*
1 teaspoon paprika	*1 teaspoon paprika*
2 fl oz chicken stock or $\frac{1}{2}$ a chicken stock cube	*60 ml chicken stock or $\frac{1}{2}$ a chicken stock cube*
2 teaspoons tomato purée	*2 teaspoons tomato purée*
2 fl oz natural low fat yogurt	*60 ml natural low fat yogurt*

Heat the grill. Brush the chicken joints with a little oil and cook under a medium heat for 10 minutes each side.

Meanwhile, heat the margarine in a frying pan, chop the onion and fry gently for 3 minutes. Crush the garlic with a little salt and add with the paprika. Add the stock, or crumble in the stock cube and add 2 fl oz (60 ml) water. Stir in the tomato purée, mix well and add salt and pepper to taste. Simmer gently while the chicken is cooking.

Lower the heat and stir in the yogurt. Place the chicken joints in the sauce, spooning it over them to baste well and leave over a very low heat for 3 or 4 minutes before serving. Do not allow the yogurt to boil.

Chicken with Fresh Tomatoes
TIME 30 minutes   SERVES 2
CALORIES PER PORTION 365

1 oz polyunsaturated margarine	*30 g polyunsaturated margarine*
1 tablespoon polyunsaturated oil	*1 tablespoon polyunsaturated oil*
2 chicken joints	*2 chicken joints*
salt and pepper	*salt and pepper*
1 medium onion (4 oz)	*1 medium onion (125 g)*
4 large tomatoes	*4 large tomatoes*
1 clove garlic	*1 clove garlic*
1 tablespoon chopped parsley	*1 tablespoon chopped parsley*

In a kettle, boil enough water to cover the tomatoes. Meanwhile, heat the margarine and oil in a lidded sauté pan. Rub the chicken joints with a little salt and pepper and fry gently for 5 minutes on each side. Meanwhile, slice the onion thinly and place the tomatoes in a bowl, covering with boiling water. Skin and chop roughly. Crush the garlic with a little salt, and chop the parsley.

Add the onions to the chicken and cook for 3 minutes. Then add the tomatoes with the garlic and parsley. Cover and simmer gently until the end of the cooking time, about 15 more minutes.

Chicken with Apple Sauce

TIME 30 minutes   SERVES 4
CALORIES PER PORTION 340

½ pint chicken stock or 1 chicken stock cube

4 chicken joints

1 teaspoon corn oil

1 oz polyunsaturated margarine

1 medium onion (4 oz)

4 oz mushrooms

1 tablespoon flour

5 fl oz dry white wine

2 cooking apples

300 ml chicken stock or 1 chicken stock cube

4 chicken joints

1 teaspoon corn oil

30 g polyunsaturated margarine

1 medium onion (125 g)

125 g mushrooms

1 tablespoon flour

150 ml dry white wine

2 cooking apples

Heat the stock or, if using a stock cube, boil ½ pint (300 ml) of water in a kettle. Brush the chicken joints with a little oil and grill under a medium heat for 12 minutes each side. Meanwhile, melt the margarine in a sauté pan. Slice the onion and cook gently while washing and slicing the mushrooms. Add these to the pan. Sprinkle with the flour and mix well.

Dissolve the stock cube in the boiling water and add. Or pour in the heated stock. Add the wine. Skin, core and slice the apples and stir in gently. Season to taste, cover and simmer for 15–20 minutes or until the chicken is cooked through. Stir the mixture thoroughly – the apples should have become pulpy and thick – and pour over the chicken.

Chicken with Mushrooms and Yogurt

TIME 20 minutes   SERVES 2
CALORIES PER PORTION 520

You don't *have* to thicken yogurt with cornflour. You can add it at the end of cooking, if you don't boil it. But if you do have problems with cooking yogurt, this method helps.

4 fl oz natural low fat yogurt	125 ml natural low fat yogurt
1 teaspoon cornflour	1 teaspoon cornflour
1½ oz polyunsaturated margarine	40 g polyunsaturated margarine
2 chicken breasts	2 chicken breasts
flour, salt and pepper	flour, salt and pepper
4 oz mushrooms	125 g mushrooms
½ teaspoon lemon rind	½ teaspoon lemon rind
4–6 fl oz chicken stock or 1 chicken stock cube	125–175 ml chicken stock or 1 chicken stock cube

Boil ½ pint (300 ml) of water in a kettle to dissolve the stock cube, if used. Place the yogurt in a small pan. Mix the cornflour with a little water to make a smooth cream. Bring the yogurt just to simmering point, add the cornflour and lower the heat. Mix well and allow to thicken while preparing the chicken. Put a plate to warm.

Heat ½ oz (15 g) margarine in a sauté pan. Dust the chicken breasts with a little flour and salt and fry in the margarine for 4 minutes each side. Remove to the warm plate.

Add the remaining margarine to the pan. Wipe and slice the mushrooms and fry for 2 minutes. Sprinkle in 1 level tablespoon flour. Grate ½ teaspoon of lemon rind and add with the yogurt and enough chicken stock to make a pouring sauce. Adjust the seasoning and pour over the chicken.

Indian Spiced Chicken

TIME 15 minutes plus overnight marinade   SERVES 4
CALORIES PER PORTION 258

1 tablespoon mustard seeds	1 tablespoon mustard seeds
1 tablespoon garam masala	1 tablespoon garam masala
1 teaspoon cumin seeds	1 teaspoon cumin seeds
1 teaspoon chilli powder	1 teaspoon chilli powder
1-inch piece of fresh ginger	2-cm piece of fresh ginger
1 large clove garlic	1 large clove garlic
2 tablespoons chopped onion	2 tablespoons chopped onion
salt	salt

4 chicken joints	*4 chicken joints*
10 fl oz natural low fat yogurt	*300 ml natural low fat yogurt*

If you have a pestle and mortar, pound the first seven ingredients until well mixed, and add salt to taste. Otherwise, crush the peeled garlic and ginger and the onion with salt, and mix with the other spices. Skin the chicken joints and prick all over with a fork. Rub the spice mixture well into the flesh, place in a shallow dish and pour the yogurt over. Leave overnight.

Place the joints under a hot grill, pour half the yogurt marinade over and grill for 10 minutes. Turn, baste, with the remaining marinade and cook for a further 10–15 minutes until cooked through.

Pork Chops with Pineapple Sauce

TIME 25 minutes   SERVES 4
CALORIES PER PORTION 435

4 pork chops	*4 pork chops*
corn oil	*corn oil*
½ oz polyunsaturated margarine	*15 g polyunsaturated margarine*
1 small onion (2 oz)	*1 small onion (60 g)*
1 level teaspoon cornflour	*1 level teaspoon cornflour*
7 oz can crushed pineapple	*200 g can crushed pineapple*
2 tablespoons vinegar	*2 tablespoons vinegar*
1 dessertspoon soya sauce	*1 dessertspoon soya sauce*
1½ oz soft dark brown sugar	*40 g soft dark brown sugar*
salt	*salt*

Heat the grill. Remove all fat from the chops, brush with a little oil and grill under a medium heat for 10 minutes each side. Meanwhile melt the margarine in a small pan. Chop the onion and fry gently in the margarine for 3 minutes.

Place the cornflour in a bowl and mix to a smooth cream with a little water. Drain the pineapple juice into a measuring jug and make up with water, if necessary, to ¼ pint (150 ml). Add to the cornflour, and pour into the pan. Add the vinegar, soya sauce and sugar and stir with the onions until smooth and thickened. Add the pineapple, thinning if necessary with a little water, add salt to taste and spoon over the chops.

Lamb Escalopes with Mushrooms
TIME 30 minutes   SERVES 4
CALORIES PER PORTION 460

12 oz boned leg of lamb	350 g boned leg of lamb
1 egg	1 egg
2 oz fresh wholemeal breadcrumbs	60 g fresh wholemeal breadcrumbs
1 tablespoon chopped parsley	1 tablespoon chopped parsley
2 oz polyunsaturated margarine	60 g polyunsaturated margarine
1 medium onion (4 oz)	1 medium onion (125 g)
8 oz mushrooms	250 g mushrooms
salt and black pepper	salt and black pepper

Cut the lamb into ¼-inch (1-cm) slices, about 2 inches (5 cm) square. Place each one on a board, cover with a piece of greaseproof paper and beat with a rolling pin until thin and doubled in size. Beat the egg in a bowl. Grate the breadcrumbs. Chop the parsley. Put a plate to warm.

Heat 1 oz (30 g) margarine in a sauté pan. Chop the onion finely and fry gently for 3 minutes without browning. Meanwhile, wipe the mushrooms, chop and add to the pan. Fry for 2 minutes. Stir in the parsley, season to taste with salt and black pepper and place on the warm plate.

Add the remaining margarine to the pan. Dip the lamb escalopes first in the beaten egg and then in the breadcrumbs, sprinkle with salt, and fry quickly for about 3 minutes each side. Top each with a spoonful of the mushroom mixture and serve immediately.

Orange Glazed Ham

TIME 15 minutes   SERVES 4
CALORIES PER PORTION 308

4 slices gammon, ½ inch thick	*4 slices gammon, 1 cm thick*
1 orange	*1 orange*
1 oz soft brown sugar	*30 g soft brown sugar*

Heat the grill. Remove the rinds from the gammon and snip the edges of the fat. Place under a medium heat and grill for 5 minutes. Meanwhile, grate the orange rind and squeeze the juice.

Place the sugar with the orange rind and a little juice in a small saucepan and heat until the sugar melts, adding enough juice to make a thick syrupy mixture. Turn the gammon, spread with the syrup and cook for a further 3–5 minutes, or until the sugar caramelizes. Serve with noodles and broccoli (see menu section).

Strawberry Yogurt Whip

TIME 10 minutes   SERVES 4
CALORIES PER PORTION 170

I particularly like strawberries and raspberries with yogurt, but you can layer this mixture with bananas, or any soft fruit you prefer.

4 egg whites	*4 egg whites*
1 pint natural low fat yogurt	*600 ml natural low fat yogurt*
8 oz fresh strawberries	*250 g fresh strawberries*
2 oz caster sugar	*60 g caster sugar*

Beat the egg whites until stiff and fold in the yogurt. Place a layer of the yogurt mixture in the base of each of 4 individual glass dishes. Slice a few strawberries on top and sprinkle with sugar. Reserve 4 whole strawberries for the top.

Repeat the layers, finishing with yogurt. Pace a whole strawberry in the centre of each dish and serve immediately or chill until required.

Mocha Fluff
TIMES 30 minutes, plus overnight setting   SERVES 4
CALORIES PER PORTION 80

To make a real mousse you should leave the gelatine mixture almost
to setting point before whisking in to the other ingredients. If you
don't, the mixture separates, and in this case it doesn't really matter
if you get a three-layer effect – jelly in the bottom, cream in the
middle and froth on top – it may not be correct enough for a party,
but is pretty enough for a family meal.

½ oz sachet gelatine	15 g sachet gelatine
1 level tablespoon instant coffee	1 level tablespoon instant coffee
1 tablespoon drinking chocolate powder	1 tablespoon drinking chocolate powder
1 tablespoon rum	1 tablespoon rum
2 egg whites	2 egg whites
5 oz natural low fat yogurt	150 ml natural low fat yogurt
liquid sweetener	liquid sweetener

Place a bowl containing 4 tablespoons of cold water over a pan of
simmering water and sprinkle in the gelatine. Stir until dissolved
and remove from the heat.

Place the coffee and chocolate powder in a cup, add a tablespoon of
the boiling water to dissolve and add to the gelatine mixture with
the rum. Make up to ½ pint (300 ml) with cold water, and place in
the fridge for 15 minutes to chill.

Whisk the egg whites until stiff, add the coffee mixture, still
beating, and finally whisk in the yogurt. Sweeten to taste and pour
into 4 individual glasses. Chill overnight.

PUDDINGS

I find puddings a paradox. The more elaborate and tempting they look the more disappointing they often turn out to be. The lighter and frothier they seem, the heavier they lie upon what has gone before. The sight of one of those amazing cream-laden trolleys in a restaurant, wheeled in after a couple of already too-rich courses (for who can be wise when having a treat?) is, to my mind, too much for any but the stout-hearted and certainly for the potentially stout. Our revelling ancestors had the right idea when they interspersed their innumerable courses with a simple sorbet to aid digestion.

However, that is the very subjective view of one who has resisted gourmet temptation too infrequently and is feeling guilty. In the south of the country there is a swing to starters rather than afters, even in a two-course family meal, and you will always get sophisticated protests from the slim and would-be slim when puddings appear. Not, however, from men, most of whom still manage to tuck into profiteroles like deprived schoolboys.

But elsewhere, puddings are definitely an English speciality. In fact, if we served nothing but breakfast and pudding we would have a much better gastronomic reputation.

There is, unfortunately, no place in quick cookery for the steamed and the baked pud, but pastry is possible – make your own short-crust when you have time and freeze it in handy, rolled-out sizes, or buy puff pastry in packets. The biscuit crust given on page 166 is a useful stand-by, as it will turn any of the gelatine-based mousses into a more filling family pud.

Otherwise, puddings divide themselves into the hot or cold sort that you make and eat immediately, and the overnight sort that need to be left to set or freeze.

Apple Marsala

TIME 30 minutes plus chilling   SERVES 4

rind of 1 orange	*rind of 1 orange*
4 oz sugar	*125 g sugar*
4 large dessert apples	*4 large dessert apples*
8 cloves	*8 cloves*
2 tablespoons Marsala	*2 tablespoons Marsala*
1 oz sultanas	*30 g sultanas*
5 fl oz whipping cream	*150 ml whipping cream*

Grate the rind of the orange and place in a saucepan just large enough to hold the apples. Add the sugar and 5 fl oz (150 ml) water and simmer until the sugar has dissolved.

Meanwhile, peel and core the apples, keeping them whole. Stick two cloves into each and place in the syrup, basting well. Cover and simmer very gently for 5–8 minutes until the apples are just soft but still whole. Place each apple in an individual glass dish.

Add the Marsala to the syrup in the pan and boil rapidly for about 5 minutes until reduced to about 6 tablespoons. Meanwhile, fill the apple cavities with sultanas. Pour the syrup over the apples and chill thoroughly. Serve with whipped cream.

Omelette Grand Marnier

TIME 15 minutes   SERVES 2

1 ripe peach	*1 ripe peach*
1 oz butter	*30 g butter*
4 eggs	*4 eggs*
5 teaspoons caster sugar	*5 teaspoons caster sugar*
1 tablespoon Grand Marnier	*1 tablespoon Grand Marnier*

Boil enough water to cover the peach. Place it in a bowl, pour boiling water over and skin, halve and cut into slices. Melt half the butter in a small pan, add the peach slices and heat gently.

Meanwhile, separate the eggs. Beat the egg yolks with 1 table-spoon of cold water until frothy. At this point put the remaining butter into a large omelette pan to melt over a very gentle heat. Heat the grill.

Whisk the egg whites in a separate bowl until stiff. Whisk four teaspoons of sugar into the egg yolks and fold in the white. Do not overmix.

Pour into the omelette pan and cook gently for 5 minutes until the underside is golden. Place under the grill very quickly to dry out the top slightly. Place the peach slices on one half, pour the Grand Marnier over, sprinkle with the remaining sugar and fold over. Serve immediately.

Hot Blackcurrant Crisp
TIME 30 minutes   SERVES 4

1 lb frozen blackcurrants	*500 g frozen blackcurrants*
7 tablespoons sugar	*7 tablespoons sugar*
4 oz cake crumbs (Victoria sponge or Madeira)	*125 g cake crumbs (Victoria sponge or Madeira)*
4 oz fresh white breadcrumbs	*125 g fresh white breadcrumbs*
2 oz butter	*60 g butter*
½ pint whipping cream	*300 ml whipping cream*

Heat the oven to Gas 5; 375° F; 190° C.

Place the blackcurrants in a saucepan with 6 tablespoons of the sugar and 2 tablespoons of water. Simmer gently until just soft, about 5 minutes.

Meanwhile, crumble the cake and mix with the breadcrumbs and the remaining sugar. Heat the butter in a frying pan and fry the crumb mixture gently until golden. Place one third of the crumbs in a 1½-pint (1-litre) soufflé dish. Drain the blackcurrants and place half the fruit on top of the crumbs. Repeat the layers once more and top with crumbs. Place in the oven to heat through for 10 minutes before serving hot with whipped cream.

Mince and Apple Slice
TIME 30 minutes   SERVES 6

4 oz plain flour	120 g plain flour
1 level teaspoon baking powder	1 level teaspoon baking powder
pinch salt	pinch salt
1 oz butter	25 g butter
½ oz sugar	15 g sugar
4 tablespoons milk	4 tablespoons milk
14 oz jar mincemeat	400 g jar mincemeat
1 tablespoon rum	1 tablespoon rum
1 Cox's apple	1 Cox's apple
1 dessertspoon icing sugar	1 dessertspoon icing sugar

Heat the oven to Gas 7; 425° F; 220° C.

Rub the flour and baking powder with the salt, butter and sugar until like breadcrumbs and mix with enough milk to make a soft scone dough. Roll out half the quantity thinly on a floured board to fit a 7-inch (16-cm) flan tin. Mix the mincemeat with the rum and spread over the scone base. Roll out the remaining dough. Peel, core and slice the apple and arrange on the mincemeat. Top with the remaining scone dough and press down slightly. Prick with a fork and bake at the top of the oven for 15 minutes. Dust with icing sugar and serve hot or cold with cream.

Zabaglione
TIME 10 minutes   SERVES 4

4 large egg yolks	4 large egg yolks
1–2 tablespoons caster sugar	1–2 tablespoons caster sugar
4 tablespoons Marsala	4 tablespoons Marsala

Place the egg yolks in a 2-pint (1-litre) bowl with the sugar. Beat until thick and light. Place a little water in an 8-inch (20-cm) pan and bring to simmering. Place the bowl on top – the bottom must not touch the water – add the Marsala and whisk constantly until thickened, about 5 minutes. Pour immediately into four stemmed glasses and serve warm.

You can whisk the yolks for 3 minutes before starting to cook the main course and leave until you have eaten it. Then, when ready for pudding, whisk the yolks again and proceed as above.

Caramel Bananas
TIME 25 minutes   SERVES 4

4 tablespoons molasses sugar	*4 tablespoons molasses sugar*
½ oz butter	*15 g butter*
4 bananas	*4 bananas*
2 tablespoons rum	*2 tablespoons rum*
5 fl oz double cream	*150 ml double cream*

Warm a serving dish. Place the sugar in a small saucepan with 4 tablespoons of water, and boil for 3 minutes. Heat the butter in a large frying pan. Peel the bananas, split them lengthways and place in the butter. Pour on the sugar syrup and simmer very gently for 15 minutes.

Place the bananas carefully on the serving dish (lift them out with a fish slice or long spatula to avoid breaking). Stir the rum into the sauce and pour over. Serve hot with cream.

Bananas in Grand Marnier
TIME 15 minutes   SERVES 4

1½ oz soft dark brown sugar	*40 g soft dark brown sugar*
1 orange	*1 orange*
1½ oz butter	*40 g butter*
3 dessertspoons Grand Marnier	*3 dessertspoons Grand Marnier*
4 bananas	*4 bananas*

Place the sugar and 4 tablespoons of water in a large frying pan and heat gently until the sugar is melted. Meanwhile, grate the orange rind and squeeze the juice. Add to the pan with the butter and mix well. Add the Grand Marnier and simmer for 5 minutes until syrupy.

Peel the bananas and slice in half lengthways. Place in the pan, baste well and simmer gently for 3 or 4 minutes or until just soft. Serve hot.

Raspberry Syllabub
TIME 15 minutes to make, 15 minutes to chill   SERVES 6

For this one, it is useful to have a blender or processor and a sieve. You lose less of the fruit if you purée it first and then you have to sieve it to get rid of the pips.

1 lb fresh raspberries	500 g fresh raspberries
3 oz caster sugar	90 g caster sugar
1 dessertspoon lemon juice	1 dessertspoon lemon juice
½ pint double cream	300 ml double cream
4 fl oz Sauternes or other	125 ml Sauternes or other
sweet white wine	sweet white wine

Purée the raspberries and sugar in a blender or processor. Squeeze the lemon juice and stir in. Beat the cream until thick and gradually add the wine, beating constantly. Sieve the raspberry purée on to the cream and fold in lightly. Turn into 6 individual glasses and chill for 15 minutes.

Strawberry and Orange Whip
TIME 30 minutes   SERVES 4

This combination of strawberry and orange is delicious, but it does
need to be eaten soon after making. It will not keep overnight.

8 oz strawberries	*250 g strawberries*
1 small orange	*1 small orange*
5 fl oz double cream	*150 ml double cream*
3 tablespoons caster sugar	*3 tablespoons caster sugar*
2 large egg whites	*2 large egg whites*

Hull the strawberries. Grate the rind of the orange and squeeze the
juice. Whip the cream until stiff and gradually add 1 tablespoon of
juice, whisking all the time.

Rub the strawberries through a sieve, add the sugar and stir into
the cream with the orange rind. Whisk the egg whites until stiff,
but not dry, and fold in gently until completely blended. Pour into
4 individual dishes and chill for 15 minutes.

Chocolate Mousse
TIME 30 minutes   SERVES 4

1 teaspoon instant coffee	*1 teaspoon instant coffee*
3 oz Bourneville chocolate	*100 g Bourneville chocolate*
1–2 tablespoons brandy	*1–2 tablespoons brandy*
3 large eggs	*3 large eggs*
salt	*salt*

Pour a little water into a small pan and bring to simmering. Use 1
tablespoon of this water to dissolve the coffee in a cup. Break the
chocolate into a bowl, place on the pan and add the coffee and
brandy. Heat until the chocolate has melted. Mix well and remove
from the heat.

Separate the eggs. Beat the egg yolks until light and gradually
add to the chocolate, whisking until thick. Put in the fridge to cool.

Whisk the egg whites with a pinch of salt until stiff and fold into the chocolate mixture with a large metal spoon until perfectly blended. Spoon into 4 ramekins (it is very rich, so you don't need large portions) and chill until required.

Tia Maria Cream
TIME 30 minutes   SERVES 4

If you like the flavour of almonds, this is also very good made with the Italian liqueur Amaretto di Saronno.

4 eggs	*4 eggs*
2 oz caster sugar	*60 g caster sugar*
2 fl oz Tia Maria (or one miniature)	*60 ml Tia Maria (or one miniature)*
1 oz blanched almonds or hazelnuts	*25 g blanched almonds or hazelnuts*
5 fl oz whipping cream	*150 ml whipping cream*

Separate the eggs. Place the egg yolks in a large bowl and keep 3 whites in another bowl. Place a little water in an 8-inch (20-cm) pan and bring to simmering. Place the large bowl containing the yolks on top and beat with the sugar for 5 minutes until warm and frothy. The bowl must not touch the simmering water below.

Remove from the heat and pour into a cold bowl to cool quickly. Stir in the Tia Maria and put in the fridge for 5 to 10 minutes to chill. Meanwhile, chop the nuts, place on a fireproof plate and grill until golden. Whip the cream and fold into the egg yolk mixture. Whisk the 3 egg whites until stiff and fold in gently with a large metal spoon. Turn into individual glasses and sprinkle with the toasted nuts.

Cinnamon Cream

TIME 10 minutes   SERVES 4

8 oz cream cheese	*250 g cream cheese*
2 tablespoons milk	*2 tablespoons milk*
2–3 tablespoons double cream	*2–3 tabelspoons double cream*
1 tablespoon sugar	*1 tablespoon sugar*
ground cinnamon	*ground cinnamon*
2 squares plain chocolate	*2 squares plain chocolate*

Mash the cheese with a fork, gradually beating in the milk until soft
and smooth. Add the cream slowly, beating until the mixture has
a thick, clotted cream consistency.

Stir in the sugar and ½ level teaspoon cinnamon, or more to taste,
and mix well. Spoon into 4 small ramekins, grate the chocolate on
top and serve immediately or chill until required.

Pineapple Cheese

TIME 20 minutes   SERVES 4

1 small fresh pineapple or
    8 oz canned pineapple pieces
	1 small fresh pineapple or
	    250 g canned pineapple pieces

8 oz cream cheese	*250 g cream cheese*

2 tablespoons Grand Marnier
    (or one miniature)
	2 tablespoons Grand Marnier
	    (or one miniature)

4 tablespoons icing sugar	*4 tablespoons icing sugar*
3 fl oz double cream	*80 ml double cream*
8 glacé cherries	*8 glacé cherries*
1 oz roasted hazelnuts	*25 g roasted hazelnuts*

Cut the pineapple into rings, remove the skin and hard centre, and
chop. Place the cheese in a bowl and add the Grand Marnier
gradually, beating well to soften. Beat in the icing sugar. Whip the
cream and stir in. Halve the cherries and fold in with the pineapple
pieces. Spoon into 4 individual glasses and sprinkle with hazelnuts.
Chill until required.

Instant Banana Cream

TIME 5 minutes   SERVES 4
A blender or processor is needed to get the banana really creamy.

2 bananas	*2 bananas*
2 teaspoons rum	*2 teaspoons rum*
8 fl oz whipping cream	*¼ litre whipping cream*
2 teaspoons caster sugar	*2 teaspoons caster sugar*
1 oz roasted hazelnuts	*25 g roasted hazelnuts*

Skin the bananas and place in the blender or processor with the rum.
Blend until completely puréed. Meanwhile, whip the cream with
the sugar until thick. Pour the banana mixture onto the cream,
whisk in and pile into 4 individual glasses. Serve immediately,
sprinkled with hazelnuts, or chill until required.

Yogurt Chantilly

TIME 10 minutes to make, 20 to chill   SERVES 4

This is the perfect instant pudding – provided you haven't already
had a creamy course. There are also plenty of variations on the
theme – you can fold in fresh fruit or purée, or whip in an egg
white for a lighter texture. The two following recipes, as a topping
for fruit or piled into a biscuit crust, are just a start.

5 fl oz whipping cream	*150 ml whipping cream*
8–10 fl oz natural yogurt	*250–300 ml natural yogurt*
4 tablespoons soft dark brown sugar	*4 tablespoons soft dark brown sugar*

Whip the cream until just stiff. Use the lesser amount of yogurt if it
is thin. If thick, you can use up to the 10 fl oz. Fold the yogurt into
the cream gently until well mixed and spoon into 4 individual glass
dishes. Sprinkle thickly and evenly with sugar and chill. The sugar
will dissolve, making a sweet topping to the contrasting, unflavoured
base.

Mixed Fruit Cream

TIME 30 minutes   SERVES 4

3 medium oranges	*3 medium oranges*
½ lemon	*½ lemon*
2 ripe pears	*2 ripe pears*
2 Cox's apples	*2 Cox's apples*
1–2 tablespoons caster sugar	*1–2 tablespoons caster sugar*
2 tablespoons kirsch (optional)	*2 tablespoons kirsch (optional)*
1 oz sultanas	*30 g sultanas*
5 fl oz whipping cream	*150 ml whipping cream*
10 fl oz natural yogurt	*300 ml natural yogurt*
4 level tablespoons soft brown sugar	*4 level tablespoons soft brown sugar*

Peel the oranges, remove any pith and pips and halve the segments. Place in a 2½-pint (1.5-litre) glass serving dish (a soufflé-type dish with straight sides is best). Squeeze in the juice of the lemon. Peel, core and dice the pears and apples and add. Sprinkle with the caster sugar and the kirsch if used. Add the sultanas and mix well. Whip the cream until thick and fold in the yogurt. Pour over the fruit and smooth the top. Sprinkle with the soft brown sugar and chill in the fridge for 10 minutes, or for longer if wished. The fruit will not discolour overnight as it is topped with the cream.

Biscuit Cursts

SWEET DIGESTIVE CRUST
TIME 5 minutes to make, plus chilling   MAKES one 7-inch crust

Biscuit crusts are the easiest way of turning a light pudding into something more substantial for the family. You must use a loose-bottomed flan tin – it doesn't come out easily otherwise. Press the crumb mixture onto the base only if making a cheesecake, or up the sides, too, if filling with fruit and cream.

3 oz butter	90 g butter
6 oz digestive biscuits	175 g digestive biscuits
1 oz demerara sugar	30 g demerara sugar

Melt the butter in a small saucepan. Place the biscuits in a plastic bag and crush with a rolling pin. Stir into the butter with the sugar and mix well. Press into a loose-bottomed flan tin and chill until required.

GINGER CRUST

| 3 oz butter | 90 g butter |
| 6 oz ginger nuts | 175 g ginger nuts |

Proceed as above, omitting the sugar.

Instant Cheesecake

TIME 15 minutes to make, 15 minutes to chill   SERVES 4 to 6

3 oz butter	90 g butter
6 oz gingernuts	175 g gingernuts
8 oz cottage cheese	250 g cottage cheese
1 tablespoon lemon juice	1 tablespoon lemon juice
1 tablespoon caster sugar	1 tablespoon caster sugar
5 fl oz whipping cream	150 ml whipping cream
1 egg white	1 egg white
8 oz fresh strawberries or other fruit in season	250 g fresh strawberries or other fruit in season

Make the ginger biscuit crust as above and place in the fridge. Rub the cheese through a sieve and gradually beat in the lemon juice (up to 1 tablespoon to taste), making a smooth mixture. Stir in the sugar.

Whip the cream and fold in, then whip the egg white and fold that in. Spoon onto the crust and chill for 15 minutes. Meanwhile halve the strawberries and arrange on top just before serving.

Banana Cream Pie

TIME 30 minutes   SERVES 6

3 oz butter	90 g butter
6 oz digestive biscuits	175 g digestive biscuits
1 teaspoon lemon rind	1 teaspoon lemon rind
½ pint double cream	300 ml double cream
15 fl oz natural yogurt	450 ml natural yogurt
vanilla essence	vanilla essence
2 large or 3 small bananas	2 large or 3 small bananas
4 tablespoons soft dark brown sugar	4 tablespoons soft dark brown sugar

Melt the butter in a small saucepan. Place the biscuits in a plastic bag and crush with a rolling pin. Stir in the butter with the lemon rind and mix well. Turn into a 9-inch (23-cm) loose-bottomed flan tin and press down well onto the base and sides. Place in the fridge to chill.

Meanwhile, whip the cream until stiff. Fold in the yogurt with a few drops of vanilla essence to taste. Chop the bananas and stir in gently. Pour into the biscuit crust and sprinkle with the sugar. Replace in the fridge for a few minutes, until the sugar has dissolved. Or leave overnight if wished.

Blackberry Brulée

TIME 20 minutes plus setting   SERVES 6

8 oz blackberries	250 g blackberries
2½ tablespoons sugar	2½ tablespoons sugar
½ pint single cream	300 ml single cream
5 fl oz double cream	150 ml double cream

4 large egg yolks	4 large egg yolks
1 slightly rounded teaspoon cornflour	1 slightly rounded teaspoon cornflour
3 oz demerara sugar	90 g demerara sugar

Place the blackberries in the bottom of a 2-pint (1¼-litre) dish and sprinkle with 1 tablespoon of sugar – or more depending on the sweetness of the fruit.

Place a little water in an 8-inch (20-cm) pan and bring to simmering. Set a bowl on top and pour in the single and double cream. Heat until bubbles begin to appear at the edges and remove from the heat immediately. Meanwhile beat the egg yolks with the remaining sugar for about 3 minutes until thick. Beat in the cornflour. Pour onto the cream gradually, stirring until well mixed. Replace over the simmering hot water and stir constantly for about 5 minutes until the custard coats the spoon lightly. Pour over the blackberries and place in the fridge to set overnight.

When set sprinkle the top evenly with brown sugar and place under a hot grill until the sugar melts. Place in the fridge again for 5 minutes until the top is crunchy.

Belgian Chocolate Cake

TIME 30 minutes plus overnight chilling   SERVES 6–8

This is quite appallingly rich and should be served in small quantities. The texture should be fairly soft.

7 oz Bourneville chocolate	200 g Bourneville chocolate
2 tablespoons brandy or rum	2 tablespoons brandy or rum
6 oz butter	175 g butter
1 egg	1 egg
1 oz caster sugar	30 g caster sugar
2 oz glacé cherries	60 g glacé cherries
8 oz thick shortcake biscuits	250 g thick shortcake biscuits

Pour a little water into a small pan and bring to simmering. Place a bowl on top and add the chocolate broken into pieces with the brandy. Heat until melted. Melt the butter in another pan. Meanwhile beat the egg with the sugar until thick. Stir the butter gradually into the chocolate and beat well until smooth. Remove from the heat and gradually beat in the egg mixture. Halve the cherries and break the biscuits into small chunks – each finger into 7 or 8 pieces. Fold the biscuit pieces into the mixture with the cherries.

Line an 8-inch (20-cm) sandwich tin with buttered paper and spoon the mixture in. Refrigerate overnight and turn out when required.

Brandy Ginger Roll

TIME 10 minutes, chill overnight   SERVES 6

½ pint whipping cream
vanilla essence
7 oz packet ginger biscuits
3 tablespoons brandy
1 oz roasted hazelnuts

300 ml whipping cream
vanilla essence
200 g packet ginger biscuits
3 tablespoons brandy
25 g roasted hazelnuts

Whisk the cream with vanilla essence to taste until thick. Place the brandy in a saucer. Dip a gingernut quickly on each side in brandy. Place a dollop of cream (about 1 teaspoon) in the centre and place on a flat plate. Dip the next biscuit, spread with cream as before and sandwich to the previous biscuit.

Continue to pile biscuits on top of each other until likely to topple over. Turn them on their sides to make a log shape and continue until all the biscuits and half the cream are used. If any brandy remains, add to the cream and whisk again.

Place the biscuit log and cream in the fridge overnight. Just before serving, cover the log with the remaining cream and sprinkle with toasted hazelnuts.

Blackberry Cream
TIME 30 minutes plus setting   SERVES 4

This, frankly, is a cheat's version of a blackberry mousse, which takes much longer because you have to let the purée get quite cold and thick before folding in. With this quick cream the egg whites will rise to the top, leaving a thicker cream below and jelly at the bottom. But don't worry. It looks pretty and is absolutely delicious.

1 lb blackberries	*500 g blackberries*
4 oz sugar	*125 g sugar*
2 teaspoons lemon juice	*2 teaspoons lemon juice*
½ oz gelatine	*15 g gelatine*
5 fl oz double cream	*150 ml double cream*
2 egg whites	*2 egg whites*

Wash the blackberries, drain and place in a pan with the sugar. Heat to simmering. Meanwhile squeeze the lemon juice and add to the pan. Simmer until the juice runs – about 8 minutes.

Meanwhile, place a little water in a small pan and bring to simmering. Place a bowl on top containing 2 tablespoons cold water. Sprinkle on the gelatine and heat until dissolved, stirring occasionally.

Rub the blackberries through a sieve, mix with the gelatine and place in the fridge for 10 minutes.

Whip the cream until thick and in another bowl whisk the egg whites. Fold the blackberry mixture gradually into the cream and then fold in the egg whites. If the mixture is too liquid to blend evenly, whisk again. Pour into 4 glass dishes and chill for 2 hours or overnight.

Lemon Mousse
TIME 20 minutes, plus setting   SERVES 6
This is a particularly refreshing mousse as it does not contain cream.

½ oz sachet gelatine	15 g sachet gelatine
2 large lemons	2 large lemons
5 eggs	5 eggs
4–5 oz caster sugar	120–150 g caster sugar

Pour a little water into a small pan and bring to simmering. Place 2 fl oz (60 ml) cold water in a bowl, sprinkle with gelatine and set on the pan. Stir until the gelatine dissolves completely. Remove from the heat. Grate the rind of one lemon and squeeze the juice of both. Add to the gelatine, and place in the fridge to cool.

Separate the eggs. Whisk the yolks with the sugar, using the extra 1 oz (30 g) if the lemons are really big. Whisk until thick and pale yellow and then whisk in the lemon and gelatine mixture.

Beat the egg whites and fold in with a large metal spoon until well blended. Spoon into a glass serving dish and chill for 1 hour, or overnight.

Cheese Creams (Coeurs à la Crème)
TIME 15 minutes plus chilling overnight   SERVES 4

There really is no need to go to the expense of buying special heart-shaped moulds for this delicious cream cheese mixture. You can simply let it drip through muslin and serve it in spoonfuls, although of course you can't then legitimately call it coeur à la crème.

4 oz cream cheese	125 g cream cheese
1 tablespoon milk	1 tablespoon milk
5 fl oz double cream	150 g double cream
1 egg white	1 egg white
2½ fl oz soured cream	75 g soured cream
sugar	sugar

Mash the cheese with the milk and a tablespoon of double cream until soft. Then whisk the egg white until stiff. In another bowl whip the remaining double cream and the soured cream together. If you do it in this order you won't have to wash the whisk in between. A speck of cream could stop the white from whisking, whereas the white won't hurt the cream.

Beat the cream into the cheese mixture, beating at first to make sure the mixture is smooth, then stirring in gently. Stir in the egg white until well mixed.

Spoon into the centre of a square of muslin and hang from a bar in the fridge. Place a plate underneath to catch the drips. Allow to drain overnight.

Turn out into a serving dish and serve alone, sprinkled with sugar, or with fresh strawberries.

Grapefruit and Mint Sorbet
TIME 10 minutes plus freezing   SERVES 4

The texture of a sorbet is improved by whisking in a stiffly beaten egg white half-way through freezing. A food processor is perfect for this as it does the job quickly without letting the ice melt completely. You can do it by hand and if you are not able to do the whisking within 2 hours, you can let it freeze completely overnight and thaw it slightly in the fridge before beating in the white.

2 oz sugar	*60 g sugar*
1 large grapefruit	*1 large grapefruit*
1 can concentrated grapefruit juice, thawed	*1 can concentrated grapefruit juice, thawed*
2 tablespoons Crème de Menthe (1 miniature)	*2 tablespoons Crème de Menthe (1 miniature)*
1 egg white	*1 egg white*

Place the sugar in a small saucepan with ¼ pint (150 ml) water and heat gently until dissolved. Squeeze the juice from the grapefruit and place in a bowl with the grapefruit concentrate and ¼ pint (150 ml) cold water. Stir in the sugar syrup and the Crème de Menthe. Pour into two ice trays and freeze for 1–2 hours, until mushy.

Whisk the egg white until stiff and beat into the ice. Pour into a lidded bowl and freeze until required.

Tangerine Ice Cream
TIME 25 minutes plus freezing   SERVES 4

This cream ice does not need to be beaten during freezing, but the texture is better if you have time to do so.

1½ lbs tangerines	*750 g tangerines*
½ lemon	*½ lemon*
4 oz sugar	*125 g sugar*
1 egg yolk	*1 egg yolk*
½ pint double cream	*300 ml double cream*

Grate the rind of 6 tangerines, giving about 1 rounded tablespoon of rind. Squeeze the juice from all the fruit. Place the rind, tangerine juice, lemon juice and sugar in a small pan and heat until the sugar dissolves. Beat the egg yolk in a measuring jug and add the juice, making ½ pint (300 ml) liquid.

Whip the cream until just thickening. At this point you have a choice. If you are going to beat the ice cream when it is mushy, half-way through freezing, then add the juice and the bits of peel as they add flavour. If not, then strain the juice through a sieve onto the cream. (If you add the bits and don't do the half-way beat, they will sink to the bottom.)

Beat the juice into the mixture gradually. Pour into a 1½-pint (900-ml) lidded container and freeze for 2 hours until mushy. If you have to leave it longer, simply thaw a little in the fridge. Turn into a bowl, whisk well and return to the freezer until required.

Freezer Maria
TIME 15 minutes plus freezing   SERVES 4–6

2 egg yolks   *2 egg yolks*
3 tablespoons icing sugar   *3 tablespoons icing sugar*
4 oz macaroons   *125 g macaroons*
2 oz walnut pieces   *60 g walnut pieces*
2 tablespoons Tia Maria   *2 tablespoons Tia Maria*
  (1 miniature)   *(1 miniature)*
½ pint double cream   *300 ml double cream*

Beat the egg yolks. Sift in the icing sugar and beat until light and
thick. Crumble the macaroons and chop the walnuts and stir in
with the Tia Maria. Whisk the cream until just stiff and stir in,
mixing well. Spoon the mixture into a 1-pint (600-ml) bowl, cover
and freeze for at least 3 hours or overnight.

Real Strawberry Ice
TIME 20 minutes plus freezing   SERVES 6

8 oz sugar   *250 g sugar*
1 lb strawberries   *500 g strawberries*
1 lemon   *1 lemon*
2 egg whites   *2 egg whites*
10 fl oz double cream   *300 ml double cream*

Place the sugar in a small pan with 5 fl oz (150 ml) water. Heat to
boiling and simmer for 5 minutes. Meanwhile, hull the strawberries
and rub them through a sieve into a bowl (or purée in a blender or
processor). Squeeze the lemon juice and stir in. Whisk the egg whites
in a large bowl.

Add the syrup to the purée and pour this mixture slowly into the
whisked whites, beating all the time. The mixture should be thick.
Whip the cream to the same consistency and beat into the whites.
Turn into a 1½-pint (1-litre) bowl and freeze overnight.

Lemon Ice Creams
TIME 25 minutes plus freezing   SERVES 4

Lemon sorbet is often seen on menus, but a lemon ice cream is not
so usual. This one needs no stirring while freezing, and is still
beautifully smooth.

4 large lemons	*4 large lemons*
½ pint double cream	*300 ml double cream*
4 egg yolks	*4 egg yolks*
4 oz icing sugar	*120 g icing sugar*

Slice the tops off the lemons, leaving ¾ of each lemon whole.
Squeeze out as much juice as you can (it will depend on whether
the width of the top of the lemons fits over your squeezer) and
then remove the lemon flesh. The best way to do this is to run the
point of a sharp knife between the pith and the rind at the top and
then to work the flesh away with your thumb. Do the same with
the lemon tops. This will take about 5 minutes per lemon.

Squeeze the flesh or rub with a wooden spoon through a sieve
to extract as much juice as possible. Cut a small piece off the base of
each lemon and place them upright in a freezer container.

Whip the cream until just thickening. Place the egg yolks in a
bowl and sieve the icing sugar on top. Whisk well until light and
fluffy. Stir in 5 fl oz (150 ml) of lemon juice and stir in the cream
until well blended. Spoon into the lemons and place a lemon lid on
each. Cover with foil and freeze until required. Place in the fridge for
10–15 minutes to soften a little before eating.

Iced Pineapple Cream
TIME 15 minutes   SERVES 4

5 fl oz whipping cream
5 fl oz natural low fat yogurt
13¼ oz can crushed pineapple
1 tablespoon kirsch
liquid sweetener

150 ml whipping cream
150 ml natural low fat yogurt
376 g can crushed pineapple
1 tablespoon kirsch
liquid sweetener

Whip the cream until thick and fold in the yogurt. Drain the pineapple in a sieve, pressing out as much syrup as possible. Stir into the
cream with the kirsch and sweetener to taste. Spoon into an ice
tray or plastic bowl and freeze for 1 hour. Mash with a fork or purée
in a blender or processor, and adjust the sweetening if required.
Serve immediately. This ice is better served soft. If you re-freeze it
overnight, soften in the fridge and mash before serving.

MENUS

Preparing and cooking more than one course in half an hour is largely a question of organization, but it needs practice, so it is best not to be too ambitious to start with. Rule one is boring but essential – you must have a tidy kitchen and one completely empty space to work on. When you are working fast any clutter is bad news. And as I am not the tidiest of cooks I can tell you it's a hard lesson, but worth learning.

The ideal, of course, is to think a day ahead or, at least, to have one or two favourites stashed in the freezer – home-made soups and ice creams are great stand-bys. You can turn a great many of the single courses in this book into three-course meals with their help. The principle of good menu-making is to vary texture and colour as well as to balance the food value of the ingredients – and although this sounds complicated you don't need to be a nutritionist to do it successfully as it is mostly common sense. You don't, for instance, serve pasta as a starter and then noodles with the meat – in fact you don't even need potatoes. If you are having a dark green vegetable, don't have a dark green soup. If the first or second course contains fruit, don't serve a fruity pudding – the same goes for cheese. And, most important, only include cream in one course. I once ran a menu-making competition which was open to professionals as well as amateurs and the number of chefs who submitted menus which included cream in every dish was amazing. A chef may be able to be extravagant, but nobody can afford to be boring, and that is the effect you will have if you ladle cream into everything.

The menus in this section are simply a guide to show how you can dovetail the preparation of different recipes in the book so that you can produce a whole meal in 30 minutes. The group of 'Instant' menus includes three courses which can be made within the time limit. The second section involves the advance preparation of one of the courses – either soup or pudding – or can be used as suggestions for instant two-course meals, if you prefer. The third section gives more ideas of what will go with what if time is no criterion.

The main course recipes can all be found under their chapter headings – sometimes a slimmer's or low-cholesterol recipe is used in a 'normal' menu to show that all the sections are flexible and suitable for all sorts of occasions. Those recipes which do not have page numbers are quick extras to show how simply one course can be padded out to make a satisfying meal.

Do read the Quick Tips on page xvii before trying your hand at 30-minute menus. It is particularly useful to have ready-prepared breadcrumbs, grated cheese, parsley and a canister of seasoned flour, all of which save valuable minutes of preparation time. It is also a good idea to make one or two of the main courses first, before trying a whole menu, so that you get used to the method of working – always assuming that you are actually working against the clock, as I was. If you are not bothered about 5 minutes here or there, then you have no problem – just follow the method and take your time. You will still be able to achieve delicious results without wasting a single second.

Ham Rolls
Prawns Creole Style (page 35)
Rice
Bananas in Rum
(version of recipe on page 160)

HAM ROLLS

3 oz cream cheese	*85 g cream cheese*
1 dessertspoon milk	*1 dessertspoon milk*
1 oz walnuts	*25 g walnuts*
4 thin slices boiled ham	*4 thin slices boiled ham*
lettuce	*lettuce*

PRAWNS CREOLE STYLE

2 oz butter	*60 g butter*
1 large onion (6 oz)	*1 large onion (175 g)*
3 sticks celery	*3 sticks celery*
1 large green pepper	*1 large green pepper*
12 oz tomatoes	*350 g tomatoes*
1 clove garlic (optional)	*1 clove garlic (optional)*
1 tablespoon chopped parsley	*1 tablespoon chopped parsley*
salt and pepper	*salt and pepper*
6 oz peeled prawns	*175 g peeled prawns*
Tabasco sauce	*Tabasco sauce*

RICE

4 oz long grain rice	*125 g long grain rice*
salt	*salt*

BANANAS IN RUM

1 oz soft dark brown sugar	*30 g soft dark brown sugar*
2 tablespoons water	*2 tablespoons water*
1 oz butter	*30 g butter*
1 tablespoon rum	*1 tablespoon rum*
2 bananas	*2 bananas*
double cream	*double cream*

1. Boil 1½ pints (900 ml) water in the kettle. Meanwhile heat 1½ oz (45 g) butter in a sauté pan. Chop the onion finely, add to the pan and cook over a low heat for 3 minutes.

2. Chop the celery and add to the pan. Mix well and continue to cook.

3. Measure 8 fl oz (¼ litre) boiling water into a saucepan. Add the rice with 1 teaspoon of salt and cook gently until the liquid is absorbed.

4. De-seed the pepper, dice and add to the vegetables. Mix well.

5. Place the tomatoes in a bowl and cover with boiling water. Skin, chop roughly and add to the vegetables with the crushed garlic if used.

6. Chop the parsley and add, with salt and pepper to taste. Continue to cook over a medium heat.

7. Place the cream cheese for the ham rolls in a bowl, add the milk and beat until smooth. Chop the walnuts and stir in. Place a spoonful of the mixture on each thin slice of ham, roll up and place two on each plate with lettuce to garnish if wished.

8. Place the sugar for the bananas with the water in a large frying pan and heat gently until the sugar is melted. Add the butter and rum and simmer for 5 minutes until syrupy.

9. Peel the bananas and slice in half lengthways. Place in the pan, cut side down, baste well and simmer gently for 3 or 4 minutes, or until just soft.

10. Heat the remaining ½ oz (15 g) of butter in a small saucepan and toss the prawns until heated through. Add to the vegetables. Stir in Tabasco sauce to taste.

11. Keep the rice and prawns hot while eating the ham rolls. Keep the bananas hot over a very low heat and serve with cream when required.

Grilled Grapefruit
Cod in Cider Sauce (page 27)
Potato Pancake and Grilled Tomatoes
Cinnamon Cream (page 164)

GRILLED GRAPEFRUIT

1 large grapefruit	*1 large grapefruit*
2 dessertspoons medium sherry	*2 dessertspoons medium sherry*
2 tablespoons soft dark brown sugar	*2 tablespoons soft dark brown sugar*
butter	*butter*

COD IN CIDER SAUCE

2 cod steaks	*2 cod steaks*
1 small onion (2 oz)	*1 small onion (60 g)*
half a bay leaf	*half a bayl eaf*
1 sprig parsley	*1 sprig parsley*
1 teaspoon lemon juice	*1 teaspoon lemon juice*
salt	*salt*
8 fl oz dry cider	*¼ litre dry cider*
½ oz butter	*15 g butter*
½ oz flour	*15 g flour*
1 tablespoon single cream	*1 tablespoon single cream*

POTATO PANCAKE AND GRILLED TOMATOES

½ oz butter	15 g butter
1 teaspoon corn oil	1 teaspoon corn oil
1 small onion (2 oz)	1 small onion (60 g)
8 oz cold mashed potato	250 g cold mashed potato
salt and pepper	salt and pepper
4 tomatoes	4 tomatoes
butter or oil for grilling	butter or oil for grilling

CINNAMON CREAM

4 oz cream cheese	125 g cream cheese
1 tablespoon milk	1 tablespoon milk
1 tablespoon double cream	1 tablespoon double cream
1 dessertspoon sugar	1 dessertspoon sugar
ground cinnamon	ground cinnamon
1 square plain chocolate	1 square plain chocolate

1. Place the cod steaks in a pan just large enough to hold them comfortably. Slice the onion and add with the bay leaf, parsley, lemon juice and a little salt. Pour in the cider, cover and bring to the boil. Simmer gently for 10–15 minutes, depending on the thickness of the fish.

2. Heat the grill. Put plates and dishes to warm.

3. Mash the cheese for the cinnamon cream with a fork, gradually mixing in the milk until soft and smooth. Add the cream slowly, beating until the mixture has a thick, clotted cream consistency. Stir in the sugar and ½ level teaspoon cinnamon, or more to taste, and mix well. Spoon into four small ramekins or dishes and chill until required. All this can be done in advance, if preferred.

4. Halve the grapefruit and cut round the rim. Place in a small ovenproof dish which will fit your grill pan and still allow space for the tomatoes, on the grid. Pour 1 dessertspoon sherry over each grapefruit half, sprinkle with 1 dessertspoon of soft brown sugar and dot with butter.

5. For the potato pancake, heat the ½ oz (15 g) butter and the corn

oil in a frying pan. Chop the onion finely, add to the pan and fry gently while preparing the tomatoes.

6. Halve the tomatoes and place, cut side down, on the grill grid, leaving enough space for the grapefruit dish. Dot with butter or brush with oil and sprinkle with salt. Do not replace under the grill yet.

7. Add the mashed potato to the sauté pan, mix well with the onion and salt to taste. Flatten into a thick cake and continue to cook over a gentle heat. When the underside is golden, turn and cook the other side.

8. Place the grapefruit dish next to the tomatoes and place them all under the grill. When the grapefruit is brown and bubbling, add a further dessertspoon of sugar to each half. Turn the tomatoes, brush with butter or oil, sprinkle with salt and pepper and continue to cook.

9. Strain ¼ pint (150 ml) of the liquor from the fish into a measuring jug. In a small pan melt the ½ oz (15 g) butter and sprinkle in the flour. Stir over a medium heat for 1 minute and gradually add the fish liquor, stirring until smooth and thickened. Add more liquid if necessary to make a pouring consistency. Remove from the heat, stir in the cream and adjust the seasoning to taste.

10. Pour the sauce over the fish and keep hot with the potatoes and tomatoes while the grapefruit is eaten.

11. Grate the chocolate over the cinnamon creams just before serving.

Garlic Prawns with Soured Cream
Indian Spiced Rice (page 89)
Lamb Chops and Green Salad
Fresh Pineapple with Whisky

GARLIC PRAWNS WITH SOURED CREAM

2 oz butter	*60 g butter*
2 cloves garlic	*2 cloves garlic*
salt	*salt*
12 oz peeled prawns	*350 g peeled prawns*
2 tablespoons chopped parsley	*2 tablespoons chopped parsley*
5 fl oz soured cream	*150 ml soured cream*

INDIAN SPICED RICE

22 fl oz chicken stock or 2 chicken stock cubes	*650 ml chicken stock or 2 chicken stock cubes*
1 oz butter	*30 g butter*
1 medium onion (4 oz)	*1 medium onion (125 g)*
1 large clove garlic	*1 large clove garlic*
salt	*salt*
1 teaspoon cumin seeds	*1 teaspoon cumin seeds*
6 whole cardamoms	*6 whole cardamoms*
3 cloves	*3 cloves*
½ teaspoon ground ginger	*½ teaspoon ground ginger*
½ inch cinnamon stick	*1 cm cinnamon stick*
12 oz long grain rice	*350 g long grain rice*

LAMB CHOPS AND GREEN SALAD

1 lettuce	1 lettuce
1 bunch watercress	1 bunch watercress
salt and black pepper	salt and black pepper
1 tablespoon wine vinegar	1 tablespoon wine vinegar
3 tablespoons corn oil	3 tablespoons corn oil
4 lamb chops	4 lamb chops

FRESH PINEAPPLE WITH WHISKY

1 small pineapple	1 small pineapple
4 teaspoons caster sugar	4 teaspoons caster sugar
4-6 teaspoons whisky	4-6 teaspoons whisky
(or kirsch if you have it)	(or kirsch if you have it)

1. Heat the chicken stock for the rice, or boil 22 fl oz (650 ml) water in a kettle if using stock cubes. Melt the butter in a large saucepan. Meanwhile, chop the onion finely and fry in the butter for 3 minutes.

2. Crush the garlic with a little salt and add with the cumin, cardamom, cloves, ginger, cinnamon stick and rice. Mix well until the rice looks transparent.

3. Dissolve the stock cube in the boiling water and add, or add the home-made stock with 1 level teaspoon salt. Allow to bubble, un-covered, until the liquid is just resting on top of the rice. Cover and continue to simmer until all the liquid is absorbed – about 15 minutes. Heat the grill and warm two dishes.

4. Wash the lettuce and watercress and place the leaves in a bowl.

5. Place ½ teaspoon of salt and a little ground black pepper in a screw top jar. Add 1 tablespoon of wine vinegar and 3 tablespoons of corn oil and shake until well mixed.

6. Sprinkle the chops with a little salt and pepper, place under the grill and cook for about 5–8 minutes each side, according to thick-ness.

7. Prepare the pineapple by cutting into ½-inch (1-cm) slices. Re-move the skin and core. Place the slices on individual plates, sprinkle

each slice with 1 teaspoon of sugar and the whisky or kirsch. Place in the fridge to chill.

8. Melt the butter for the prawns in a sauté pan. Crush the garlic with a little salt and add. Heat gently – do not allow the garlic to brown. Add the prawns and shake in the butter until hot. Stir in the parsley and soured cream – do not allow to boil.

9. Toss the salad in the dressing. Divide the prawns between 4 individual ramekins or small dishes and keep the chops and rice hot while eating the first course.

Low-Cholesterol Menu

Pepper Salad
(page 117, using polyunsaturated margarine)
Lamb Escalopes with Mushrooms (page 153)
Noodles
Raspberry Yogurt Whip (page 154)

PEPPER SALAD

½ oz polyunsaturated margarine	*15 g polyunsaturated margarine*
1 dessertspoon corn oil	*1 dessertspoon corn oil*
2 medium onions (each 4 oz)	*2 medium onions (each 125 g)*
1 large green pepper	*1 large green pepper*
2 large red peppers	*2 large red peppers*
4 tomatoes	*4 tomatoes*
1 clove garlic	*1 clove garlic*
salt and black pepper	*salt and black pepper*

LAMB ESCALOPES WITH MUSHROOMS

2 oz polyunsaturated margarine	*60 g polyunsaturated margarine*
1 medium onion (4 oz)	*1 medium onion (125 g)*
8 oz mushrooms	*250 g mushrooms*
1 tablespoon chopped parsley	*1 tablespoon chopped parsley*
salt and black pepper	*salt and black pepper*
1 egg	*1 egg*
2 oz fresh wholemeal breadcrumbs, already grated	*60 g fresh wholemeal breadcrumbs, already grated*
12 oz boned leg of lamb	*350 g boned leg of lamb*

NOODLES

12 oz noodles	*350 g noodles*
salt	*salt*

RASPBERRY YOGURT WHIP

4 egg whites	*4 egg whites*
1 pint natural low fat yogurt	*600 ml natural low fat yogurt*
8 oz fresh raspberries	*250 g fresh raspberries*
2 oz caster sugar	*60 g caster sugar*

1. Boil 1 pint (600 ml) water in the kettle and put a large pan of water on to boil for the noodles

2. Heat the margarine and oil for the pepper salad in a large sauté pan. Slice the two medium onions for the pepper salad and fry gently without browning for 3 minutes. De-seed the peppers and cut into thin strips 2 inches (5 cm) long. Add to the onions, mix well and cook for 5 minutes.

3. Heat 1 oz (30 g) of the margarine for the lamb escalopes in a saucepan. Chop the other onion finely and fry gently without browning.

4. Meanwhile place the tomatoes in a bowl, cover with boiling water, skin and chop roughly. Add to the peppers. Crush the garlic with a little salt and add. Mix well, season to taste, cover and continue to cook gently.

5. Add the noodles to the pan of water when boiling. Add 1 teaspoon of salt and cook for about 8–10 minutes until tender. Put a serving dish to warm.

6. Wipe the mushrooms and chop roughly – this can be done with a large cook's knife or carving knife to save time. Add to the onion in the saucepan. Add the parsley and salt and black pepper to taste. Cook over a medium heat.

7. Add the remaining 1 oz (30 g) margarine to a frying pan. Beat the egg in a bowl and place the breadcrumbs on a plate. Cut the lamb into $\frac{1}{4}$-inch (1-cm) slices, about 2 inches (5 cm) square, place on a board and cover with greaseproof paper. Beat with a rolling pin until thin and double in size. Dip the escalopes first in the egg and then in the breadcrumbs, sprinkle with salt and fry quickly for about 3 minutes each side.

8. Whip the egg whites until stiff and fold in the yogurt. Place a layer of the mixture in the base of each of 4 individual dishes. Divide the raspberries between the dishes, leaving a few for decoration. (Raspberries are used in this menu because they do not need time to hull, but you can use whatever fruit you prefer or have time for.) Sprinkle with sugar and top with the remaining yogurt mixture. Place in the fridge to chill.

9. Place the lamb on the warm dish and top with the mushroom mixture. Keep this and the drained noodles warm while eating the hot pepper salad.

10. Decorate the yogurt with the remaining raspberries just before serving.

Shrimp Filled Tomatoes
Lamb Chops with Swiss Cheese (page 69)
Broccoli with Almonds (page 93)
Rice
Brandied Peaches

SHRIMP FILLED TOMATOES

4 large tomatoes	*4 large tomatoes*
5 fl oz thick mayonnaise	*150 ml thick mayonnaise*
1 teaspoon tomato purée	*1 teaspoon tomato purée*
Tabasco sauce	*Tabasco sauce*
4 oz peeled prawns	*125 g peeled prawns*
salt and black pepper	*salt and black pepper*
lettuce	*lettuce*

LAMB CHOPS WITH SWISS CHEESE

4 lamb chump chops	*4 lamb chump chops*
4 oz Emmenthal or Gruyère cheese	*100 g Emmenthal or Gruyère cheese*
1 clove garlic	*1 clove garlic*
salt	*salt*
½ oz butter	*15 g butter*

BROCCOLI WITH ALMONDS

1½ lbs broccoli	*750 g broccoli*
salt and black pepper	*salt and black pepper*
2 oz butter	*50 g butter*
2 oz blanched whole almonds	*50 g blanched whole almonds*
1 teaspoon lemon juice	*1 teaspoon lemon juice*

RICE

8 oz long grain rice   *250 g long grain rice*
salt   *salt*

BRANDIED PEACHES

4 ripe peaches   *4 ripe peaches*
4 oz butter   *125 g butter*
2 oz sugar   *60 g sugar*
4 tablespoons brandy   *4 tablespoons brandy*

1. Boil 2 pints (1·25 litres) water in the kettle. Heat the grill. Put plates and dishes to warm for the chops, broccoli and rice.
2. Trim the broccoli, discarding the tough ends of the stalks. Wash the lettuce leaves for the tomatoes – a couple each for garnish.
3. Slit the chops horizontally to the bone. Cut 4 small, thick slices of cheese about 1 oz (25 g) each and place in the slits like a sandwich filling. Fold the cheese if necessary, to fit the pockets exactly.
4. Measure 15 fl oz (450 ml) boiling water into a saucepan, add the rice and a teaspoon of salt and cook uncovered, until the water is bubbling on the surface. Cover and simmer gently until the liquid is absorbed.
5. Meanwhile crush the garlic with a little salt and rub both sides of the chops. Dot with butter and cook under a medium heat for 5–8 minutes each side, depending on thickness.
6. Pour about 1 inch (2 cm) depth of water into an 8-inch (20-cm) pan. Add ½ teaspoon of salt and the broccoli. Cover and simmer for 8–10 minutes or until just tender.
7. Halve the tomatoes and scoop out the seeds. Place the mayonnaise in a bowl and add the tomato purée and Tabasco to taste. Stir in the prawns, add salt and pepper to taste and pile into the tomato halves. Place the lettuce leaves on 4 individual plates and top with 2 stuffed tomato halves each.
8. Melt the 2 oz (50 g) butter for the broccoli in a pan and fry the almonds until golden.
9. Place the peaches in a bowl and pour the remaining boiling water

over. Leave for 1 minute and remove skins. Halve and remove stones.

10. Heat the butter for the peaches in a sauté pan large enough to take the 8 halves. Add the sugar and brandy and heat until dissolved. Place the peaches cut side down in the mixture and heat gently, basting the peaches well.

11. Drain the broccoli, add the almonds and their butter with the teaspoon of lemon juice and turn until well mixed. Sprinkle with black pepper. Turn the peaches and baste again with the syrup.

12. Keep the chops, broccoli and rice hot while eating the tomatoes. The peaches may continue to cook very gently until required.

Tagliatelle with Butter and Parmesan
Chicken with Red Peppers (page 125)
Cauliflower Purèe (page 96)
Melon with White Wine and Blackberries*

TAGLIATELLE WITH BUTTER AND PARMESAN

12 oz tagliatelle	*350 g tagliatelle*
salt and black pepper	*salt and black pepper*
3 oz butter	*90 g butter*
3 oz grated Parmesan cheese	*90 g grated Parmesan cheese*

CHICKEN WITH RED PEPPERS

2 tablespoons corn oil	*2 tablespoons corn oil*
4 chicken joints	*4 chicken joints*
2 medium onions (each 4 oz)	*2 medium onions (each 125 g)*
2 red peppers	*2 red peppers*
1 lb tomatoes	*500 g tomatoes*
1 large clove garlic	*1 large clove garlic*
salt and black pepper	*salt and black pepper*

CAULIFLOWER PURÉE

1 large cauliflower	*1 large cauliflower*
salt and black pepper	*salt and black pepper*
1 oz butter	*30 g butter*
2 tablespoons single cream	*2 tablespoons single cream*
nutmeg	*nutmeg*

MELON WITH WHITE WINE AND BLACKBERRIES*

2 small melons – ogen or similar size	*2 small melons – ogen or similar size*
8 oz blackberries	*250 g blackberries*
3 fl oz Sauternes or other sweet white wine	*80 ml Sauternes or other sweet white wine*
2 tablespoons caster sugar	*2 tablespoons caster sugar*

* The melon is also particularly delicious stuffed with large green grapes and steeped in Muscatel wine. Sweet white wine will stay in good condition for at least a week after opening, but as you only need a small quantity for this recipe you may like the excuse to round off the meal with the rest of the bottle.

1. Boil 1 pint (600 ml) water in the kettle. Heat a large pan of water for the tagliatelle. Heat 1 tablespoon of oil in a deep sauté pan and brown the chicken joints on both sides. Reduce the heat and cook gently while preparing the rest of the meal. Turn half way through the cooking time.

2. Heat the remaining tablespoon of oil in a saucepan. Slice the onions and fry in this oil gently for 3 minutes. De-seed and slice the peppers and add to the onions. Mix well and continue to cook.

3. Heat 1 inch (2 cm) depth of water in a saucepan for the cauliflower.

4. Remove the outer leaves from the cauliflower and divide into florets. Add to the saucepan with ½ teaspoon of salt. Cover and simmer for 10 minutes, or until just tender. Warm dishes for the chicken and cauliflower.

5. Place the tomatoes in a bowl and cover with boiling water. Crush the garlic with a little salt. Skin the tomatoes, chop roughly

and add to the peppers and onions with the garlic and seasoning to taste. Cook until the tomatoes are soft and then pour over the chicken joints. Continue to cook gently.

6. Halve the melons, scoop out the seeds, cut a piece off the base of each half so that they sit firmly and place each on an individual plate. Divide the blackberries between the halves, piling in the centres. Pour the wine over the berries. Place in the fridge until required.

7. Drain the cauliflower and place in a blender or processor. Add the butter and cream and blend. Return to the pan, adjust the seasoning and add grated nutmeg to taste. Heat through gently.

8. Drain the tagliatelle and return to the pan with the butter and salt and pepper to taste. Toss until the butter is melted. Place the chicken and cauliflower in the warmed dishes and keep hot. Serve the tagliatelle with the Parmesan handed separately.

9. Sprinkle the blackberries with the caster sugar just before serving.

Baked Avocados with Crab (page 13)
Chicken with Walnuts on Rice (page 48)
Strawberry Yogurt Cream

BAKED AVOCADOS WITH CRAB

1 oz butter	*30 g butter*
1 tablespoon chopped onion	*1 tablespoon chopped onion*
4 oz crabmeat, fresh or canned	*125 g crabmeat, fresh or canned*
2 tablespoons ready-prepared fresh white breadcrumbs	*2 tablespoons ready-prepared fresh white breadcrumbs*
1–2 tablespoons single cream	*1–2 tablespoons single cream*
2 ripe avocados	*2 ripe avocados*
salt and pepper	*salt and pepper*
paprika	*paprika*
1 oz ready-grated Cheddar cheese	*30 g ready-grated Cheddar cheese*

CHICKEN WITH WALNUTS ON RICE

12 oz long grain rice	*350 g long grain rice*
2–3 tablespoons corn oil	*2–3 tablespoons corn oil*
1 medium onion (4 oz)	*1 medium onion (125 g)*
4 oz walnut pieces	*125 g walnut pieces*
4 chicken breasts	*4 chicken breasts*
1 tablespoon cornflour	*1 tablespoon cornflour*
salt	*salt*
2 tablespoons sherry	*2 tablespoons sherry*
1 dessertspoon sugar	*1 dessertspoon sugar*
1–2 dessertspoons soya sauce	*1–2 dessertspoons soya sauce*

STRAWBERRY YOGURT CREAM

5 fl oz whipping cream	*150 ml whipping cream*
½ pint natural yogurt	*300 ml natural yogurt*
8 oz fresh strawberries	*250 g fresh strawberries*
2 oz caster sugar	*60 g caster sugar*

1. Heat the oven to Gas 6; 400° F; 200° C.
2. Measure 22 fl oz (650 ml) water into a saucepan and set over a high heat.
3. Prepare the avocados by melting the butter in a frying pan. Chop the onion finely and fry gently for 3 minutes without browning. Add the crabmeat and breadcrumbs and heat through.
4. Add the rice to the boiling water with 1 teaspoon of salt, cover and simmer gently until the liquid is absorbed.
5. Halve the avocados, remove the stones and place in a shallow ovenproof dish. Add the cream to the crab mixture with salt, pepper and paprika to taste and spoon the mixture into the cavities. Sprinkle with grated cheese and bake towards the top of the oven for 20 minutes. Place a serving dish to warm.
6. Prepare the yogurt cream. Beat the cream until stiff, then fold in the yogurt gently, until well mixed. Place a layer of the yogurt mixture in the base of 4 individual glass dishes. Slice a few strawberries on top and sprinkle with sugar. Reserve 4 strawberries for

the tops. Repeat the layers, finishing with yogurt. Place a whole strawberry in the centre of each and place in the fridge.

7. For the chicken, heat the oil in a sauté pan and meanwhile chop the onion. Add to the pan and fry gently for 2 minutes. Chop the walnuts roughly, add to the onion and fry together for 3 minutes while preparing the chicken.

8. Cut the chicken into ½-inch (1-cm) dice and toss in the cornflour mixed with a small pinch of salt. Remove the onions and walnuts to the warm dish. Add an extra tablespoon of oil to the pan if needed and fry the chicken quickly for 2 minutes, turning the pieces all the time. Add the sherry, sugar and soya sauce to taste. Return the walnuts and onions to the pan and fry, stirring, for 1 more minute.

9. Turn the rice into the warmed serving dish and pile the chicken mixture on top. Cover with foil and keep warm while eating the avocados.

Spinach Salad (page 108)
Chicken Breasts with Rice and Courgettes*
Yogurt Chantilly (page 165)

SPINACH SALAD

4 oz streaky bacon	*125 g streaky bacon*
4 oz mushrooms	*125 g mushrooms*
8–12 oz fresh spinach	*250–350 g fresh spinach*
½ teaspoon salt	*½ teaspoon salt*
black pepper	*black pepper*
2 tablespoons corn oil	*2 tablespoons corn oil*
3 teaspoons wine vinegar	*3 teaspoons wine vinegar*

CHICKEN BREASTS WITH RICE AND COURGETTES*

1 lb courgettes	*500 g courgettes*
12 oz long grain rice	*350 g long grain rice*
salt	*salt*
1 oz butter	*30 g butter*
4 chicken breasts	*4 chicken breasts*
seasoned flour (page xviii)	*seasoned flour (page xviii)*
4 oz grated Cheddar cheese	*125 g grated Cheddar cheese*

*A version of the recipe on page 47, but as you have bacon in the first course, the ham in the original chicken recipe is omitted.

YOGURT CHANTILLY

5 fl oz whipping cream	*150 ml whipping cream*
8–10 fl oz natural yogurt	*250–300 ml natural yogurt*
4 tablespoons soft dark brown sugar	*4 tablespoons soft dark brown sugar*

1. Place 22 fl oz (650 ml) of water in one saucepan and 1 inch (2 cm) depth of water in another and heat to boiling.
2. Trim and wash the courgettes, keeping them whole.
3. Add 1 teaspoon of salt and the rice to the larger quantity of water, cover and simmer until the liquid is absorbed. Add a pinch of salt and the courgettes to the other pan, cover and simmer for about 20 minutes, or until tender. Warm a plate.
4. De-rind the bacon and fry until crisp. Meanwhile wipe and chop the mushrooms. Remove the bacon and cool. Add the mushrooms to the bacon fat and fry for 2 minutes.
5. Melt the butter for the chicken in a sauté pan. Sprinkle the chicken breasts with seasoned flour and cook in the butter for 4–5 minutes each side.
6. Whip the cream for the yogurt Chantilly until just stiff. Fold in the yogurt gently until well mixed and spoon into 4 individual glass dishes. Sprinkle thickly and evenly with sugar and place in the fridge. Check the courgettes for tenderness. If done, drain. Heat the grill.

7. Wash the spinach and strip the leaves from the stems. Shake dry and tear into small pieces. Place in a bowl. Mix the salt, pepper, oil and vinegar in a cup, whisking with a fork. Crumble the bacon over the spinach and add the mushrooms and dressing. Toss well together and divide into 4 individual salad bowls.

8. Place the chicken breasts on a heatproof serving dish, sprinkle with the cheese and grill until it is melted and golden. Keep hot with the rice and courgettes while eating the spinach salad.

MENUS WITH ONE READY-PREPARED COURSE FOR TWO

Leeks Vinaigrette (page 115)
Honeyed Pork Chops (page 62)
Red Cabbage (page 146) made in advance
and Sauté Potatoes
Banana Whip

LEEKS VINAIGRETTE

4 small leeks	*4 small leeks*
½ chicken stock cube	*½ chicken stock cube*
1 small clove garlic	*1 small clove garlic*
salt and black pepper	*salt and black pepper*
1 tablespoon wine vinegar	*1 tablespoon wine vinegar*
½ teaspoon French mustard	*½ teaspoon French mustard*
4 tablespoons olive oil	*4 tablespoons olive oil*
1 dessertspoon chopped parsley	*1 dessertspoon chopped parsley*
1 dessertspoon chopped chives	*1 dessertspoon chopped chives*
1 teaspoon chopped capers	*1 teaspoon chopped capers*

HONEYED PORK CHOPS

1 small onion	*1 small onion*
2 tablespoons honey	*2 tablespoons honey*
2 tablespoons wine vinegar	*2 tablespoons wine vinegar*
Worcestershire sauce	*Worcestershire sauce*
2 thick pork chops	*2 thick pork chops*
salt	*salt*

RED CABBAGE AND SAUTÉ POTATOES

Half quantity red cabbage recipe (page 146)	*Half quantity red cabbage recipe (page 146)*
½ oz butter	*15 g butter*
1 tablespoon corn oil	*1 tablespoon corn oil*
12 oz cold boiled potatoes	*350 g cold boiled potatoes*

BANANA WHIP

5 fl oz whipping cream	*150 ml whipping cream*
5 fl oz natural yogurt	*150 ml natural yogurt*
vanilla essence	*vanilla essence*
1 banana	*1 banana*
2 tablespoons soft dark brown sugar	*2 tablespoons soft dark brown sugar*

1. Place the red cabbage, either prepared the night before, or straight from the freezer, in a saucepan over a gentle heat. Remember to stir occasionally to prevent burning.

2. Boil ½ pint (300 ml) water in the kettle. Meanwhile, chop the onion for the pork chops finely and place in a small saucepan with the honey, vinegar and a dash of Worcestershire sauce. Heat until the honey melts. Heat the grill.

3. Trim and slit the leeks half-way through lengthways and wash under running water. Cut into 2-inch (5-cm) lengths and place in a saucepan.

4. Rub the chops with salt and place them on a shallow ovenproof dish that will fit your grill pan. Pour the honey sauce over the chops

and grill under a medium heat for about 10 minutes each side, basting regularly.

5. Dissolve the stock cube in the boiling water and add to the leeks. Cover and simmer gently for 8–10 minutes until just tender.

6. Crush the garlic with a little salt and place in a screw top jar with the vinegar for the dressing. Add the mustard and olive oil and shake until blended. Chop the parsley, chives and capers all together and add to the dressing with more salt and pepper to taste.

7. Heat the $\frac{1}{2}$ oz (15 g) butter for the potatoes in a sauté pan with the tablespoon of oil. Dice the potatoes and add, frying until golden and turning to brown all sides.

8. Place the cream for the banana whip in a bowl and whip until stiff. Stir in the yogurt and add vanilla essence to taste. Peel and chop the banana and stir in. Turn the mixture into 2 individual glass dishes and sprinkle with the brown sugar. Place in the fridge until required.

9. Drain the leeks and pour the dressing over.

10. Keep the chops, cabbage and potatoes warm while eating the first course.

Corn on the Cob
Chicken Breasts in Vermouth (page 46)
Rice and Buttered Spring Greens
Lemon Ice Creams (page 176) made in advance

CORN ON THE COB

2 cobs of corn	*2 cobs of corn*
salt	*salt*
butter	*butter*

CHICKEN BREASTS IN VERMOUTH

1 medium onion (about 4 oz)	1 medium onion (about 125 g)
½ oz butter	15 g butter
1 tablespoon corn oil	1 tablespoon corn oil
2 chicken breasts	2 chicken breasts
1 tablespoon flour	1 tablespoon flour
salt and pepper	salt and pepper
5 fl oz chicken stock or 1 chicken stock cube	150 ml chicken stock or 1 chicken stock cube
3 tablespoons dry white vermouth	3 tablespoons dry white vermouth
½ teaspoon dried tarragon	½ teaspoon dried tarragon
2 tablespoons double cream	2 tablespoons double cream

RICE AND BUTTERED SPRING GREENS

4 oz long grain rice	125 g long grain rice
salt and black pepper	salt and black pepper
¾ lb spring greens	350 g spring greens
½ oz butter	15 g butter

1. Boil a kettle of water. Slice the onion. Heat the butter and oil gently in a sauté pan.

2. Place the corn cobs in a pan just big enough to hold them. Cover with boiling water and simmer for 20 minutes or until tender.

3. Dust the chicken breasts with flour mixed with a pinch of salt and a little pepper and fry in the butter and oil for about 3 minutes each side. Meanwhile, warm serving dishes for the chicken, rice and spring greens.

4. Measure 7 fl oz (200 ml) boiling water into a saucepan. Bring back to the boil, add the rice and half a teaspoon salt. Stir once, cover and simmer until the liquid is absorbed. While this is cooking, remove the centre stalks from the spring greens, wash and shred.

5. Remove the chicken from the sauté pan and place on the warmed serving dish. Add the sliced onion to the butter remaining in the pan and cook gently for 3 minutes. Pour a little water into a saucepan for the cabbage and bring to boiling.

6. Crumble the stock cube into the pan containing the onions and add $\frac{1}{4}$ pint (150 ml) hot water, or add the home-made stock. Add the vermouth and tarragon and boil rapidly for 2–3 minutes to reduce by half.

7. Add the spring greens and a pinch of salt to the boiling water in the saucepan, cover and simmer for 3–5 minutes until just tender.

8. Remove the onion mixture from the heat, stir in the cream and add salt and pepper to taste. Pour over the chicken breasts.

9. Drain the spring greens, return to the pan and add the $\frac{1}{2}$ oz (15 g) butter and a generous sprinkling of black pepper. Remove the ice cream from the freezer.

10. Keep the chicken, spring greens and rice warm in the pre-heated dishes while eating the drained corn, spread generously with butter and sprinkled with salt.

Watercress Soup (page 114)

Pork Chops with Apples and Green Beans

(page 62)

Blackberry Cream (page 171)

half quantity made in advance

WATERCRESS SOUP

$\frac{1}{2}$ oz butter	*15 g butter*
1 medium onion (4 oz)	*1 medium onion (125 g)*
2 medium potatoes	*2 medium potatoes*
1 bunch watercress	*1 bunch watercress*
15 fl oz chicken stock or 1 chicken stock cube	*450 ml chicken stock or 1 chicken stock cube*
salt and black pepper	*salt and black pepper*
2 tablespoons single cream (optional)	*2 tablespoons single cream (optional)*

PORK CHOPS WITH APPLES AND GREEN BEANS

2 loin pork chops, each ¾ inch thick	*2 loin pork chops, each 2 cm thick*
salt and pepper	*salt and pepper*
1 clove garlic	*1 clove garlic*
1 tablespoon corn oil	*1 tablespoon corn oil*
2 dessert apples	*2 dessert apples*
2 fl oz dry cider	*60 ml dry cider*
3 tablespoons chicken stock	*3 tablespoons chicken stock*
1 lb runner beans or 12 oz frozen green beans	*500 g runner beans or 350 g frozen green beans*

(As there are potatoes in the soup and you may wish to serve it with bread, no potatoes are served with the second course, but the quantity of beans is increased.)

1. Sprinkle the chops with salt and pepper. Crush the garlic and rub into the meat. Heat the corn oil in a large frying pan and brown the chops for 5 minutes each side.

2. Meanwhile, prepare the soup. If using a stock cube, boil 15 fl oz (450 ml) water in a kettle. Heat the butter in a large saucepan. Chop the onion and cook gently for 3 minutes. Scrape and dice the potatoes and cook with the onion for 2 minutes. Wash the watercress and remove the tough ends of the stems. Add to the pan. Dissolve the stock cube in the boiling water and reserve 3 tablespoons of stock for the chops. Add the remainder to the pan, cover and simmer for 10 minutes. Warm serving dishes for the pork and for the beans.

3. Peel, core and slice the apples. Push the chops to one side of the pan, add the apples and cook for a further 10–12 minutes, turning the apples so that they brown in the fat.

4. During this cooking stage, prepare the beans, removing the tops, tails and strings and then slicing. (A bean shredder does all this in one preparation.) Cook, covered, in boiling salted water for 5–8 minutes until just tender or use frozen beans, cooking for 3 minutes only.

5. Pour off any fat from the chops and place the meat in the warmed serving dish, topped with the apples.

6. Add the cider to the frying pan, mixing well with any brown sticky bits. Add the 3 tablespoons of chicken stock and boil up quickly for 3 minutes until reduced to a thin sauce. Pour over the chops and keep hot. Drain the beans and place in a serving dish.
7. Purée the soup in a blender or processor, adjust the seasoning and stir in the cream just before serving.

MENUS WITH ONE READY-PREPARED COURSE FOR FOUR

Hot Stuffed Tomatoes (page 139)
Lemon Pork with Mushrooms and Noodles
(page 66)
Mocha Fluff (page 155) made in advance

HOT STUFFED TOMATOES

1 tablespoon corn oil	1 tablespoon corn oil
½ oz polyunsaturated margarine	15 g polyunsaturated margarine
1 medium onion (4 oz)	1 medium onion (125 g)
6 large tomatoes	6 large tomatoes
4 oz fresh wholemeal breadcrumbs, ready grated	125 g fresh wholemeal breadcrumbs, ready grated
2 tablespoons chopped parsley	2 tablespoons chopped parsley
1 oz stuffed olives	25 g stuffed olives
salt and pepper	salt and pepper

LEMON PORK WITH MUSHROOMS AND NOODLES

12 oz pork fillet	350 g pork fillet
1 egg	1 egg

3 tablespoons flour	*3 tablespoons flour*
salt and black pepper	*salt and black pepper*
1 tablespoon cooking oil	*1 tablespoon cooking oil*
3 oz butter	*90 g butter*
4 oz mushrooms	*125 g mushrooms*
½ lemon	*½ lemon*
8 oz noodles	*250 g noodles*
2 Cox's apples	*2 Cox's apples*

1. Heat the oven to Gas 6; 400° F; 200° C. Put a large pan of water on to boil for the noodles.

2. Heat the oil and margarine for the tomatoes in a saucepan. Chop the onion and fry gently for 3 minutes without browning. Meanwhile, halve the tomatoes and scoop out the centres. Place the tomato cases on a baking tray. Add the tomato pulp to the onions with the breadcrumbs and parsley.

3. Chop the olives finely and add to the mixture with salt and pepper to taste. Mix well and spoon into the tomato halves. Although this recipe comes from the low-cholesterol section, this meal is not intended for cholesterol watchers, and you may therefore dot the tomatoes with butter, if you wish. Place the tomatoes towards the top of the oven and bake while cooking the rest of the meal. Warm a dish for the noodles and pork.

4. Cut the pork into strips 2 inches × ½ inch (5 cm × 1 cm). Beat the egg, and sprinkle the flour, seasoned with a little salt and black pepper, on a board. Heat the oil and 2 oz (60 g) butter in a sauté pan. Dip the pork strips first in the beaten egg and then in the flour and fry for 5 minutes, turning to cook all sides.

5. Meanwhile, wipe and slice the mushrooms. Add these to the pork and fry for 2 minutes. Squeeze the lemon and pour the juice into the pan. Add salt and pepper to taste, mixing well. Leave on a low heat.

6. Add the noodles to the pan of water with 1 teaspoon salt and boil for 5–8 minutes until just tender.

7. Heat the remaining 1 oz (30 g) butter in a frying pan. Peel the apples, leaving them whole, core and cut into rings. Fry in the butter over a fairly high heat for 2 minutes each side, until golden.

8. Arrange the drained noodles round the edge of the warmed

serving dish and pile the pork in the middle, topping with the apples. Keep warm while eating the stuffed tomatoes.

Carrot Soup with Dill (page 138)
made in advance or from the freezer
Lamb's Liver in Butter,
or Grilled Lamb Chops
(if you don't like liver)
Spinach with Pine Kernels (page 18)
Sauté Potatoes
Baked Stuffed Apples

LAMB'S LIVER IN BUTTER

2 oz butter	*60 g butter*
8 thin slices lamb's liver or 4 lamb chops	*8 thin slices lamb's liver or 4 lamb chops*
flour	*flour*
salt and black pepper	*salt and black pepper*
1 tablespoon chopped parsley	*1 tablespoon chopped parsley*

SPINACH WITH PINE KERNELS

1 lb frozen leaf spinach	*500 g frozen leaf spinach*
2 rashers smoked back bacon	*2 rashers smoked back bacon*
1 oz butter	*30 g butter*
1 medium onion (4 oz)	*1 medium onion (125 g)*
1 oz pine kernels	*25 g pine kernels*
1 clove garlic	*1 clove garlic*
lemon juice	*lemon juice*
salt and black pepper	*salt and black pepper*

SAUTÉ POTATOES

1 oz butter	*30 g butter*
1 tablespoon corn oil	*1 tablespoon corn oil*
1 lb cold boiled potatoes	*500 g cold boiled potatoes*
(1½ lbs uncooked)	*(750 g uncooked)*

BAKED STUFFED APPLES

4 small cooking apples	*4 small cooking apples*
(each 4 oz)	*(each 125 g)*
2 oz sultanas	*50 g sultanas*
4 teaspoons brown sugar	*4 teaspoons brown sugar*
butter	*butter*

1. Heat the oven to Gas 6; 400° F; 200° C. Core the apples and make a horizontal slit almost all the way round the circumference of each. Place in a shallow ovenproof dish and spoon sultanas into the cored spaces. Press down and spoon the sugar on top. Pour 4 tablespoons water over the apples and dot with a little butter. Place the dish towards the top of the oven and bake until required.

2. Place the frozen spinach in a saucepan with 1 tablespoon water and heat gently.

3. Place the carrot soup in a saucepan over a low heat.

4. De-rind the bacon and cut into very small strips. Heat the 1 oz (30 g) butter for the spinach recipe in a saucepan and fry the bacon over a medium heat. Meanwhile chop the onion finely, add to the bacon and continue to fry for 2 or 3 minutes until the bacon is crisp.

5. Heat the butter and oil for the potatoes in a large frying pan and cut the cold potatoes into ¼-inch (1-cm) slices. Add to the frying pan and sauté until golden on both sides.

6. Meanwhile place the pine kernels on a heatproof plate and brown under the grill. If cooking chops, place them under the grill when the pine kernels are finished and cook for 5–8 minutes each side, according to thickness. Warm a plate and dishes for the liver (or chops) and vegetables.

7. Turn the spinach into a sieve and press out as much water as possible. Return the spinach to the pan. Crush the garlic with a little

salt and add with the bacon and onion. Add a squeeze of lemon juice and salt and black pepper to taste and mix well, separating the spinach leaves carefully.

8. Add the 2 oz (60 g) butter for the liver to the pan just used for the bacon and onion and heat gently. Place the liver slices on a board and sprinkle generously with flour mixed with a little salt and pepper. Place the liver in the pan and fry quickly for 2 minutes each side. Place on the warmed plate. Sprinkle the parsley into the pan, swirl round and pour the herby butter over the liver.

9. Keep the liver, potatoes and spinach hot while drinking the soup. By the time the first two courses have been eaten, the apples will be ready. Spoon the syrup in the bottom of their dish over each and serve with cream or on their own.

Spaghetti with Oil and Garlic
Spiced Meatballs (page 60)
Sweet and Sour Chinese Cabbage (page 95)
Lemon Mousse (page 172) made in advance

SPAGHETTI WITH OIL AND GARLIC

12 oz spaghetti	*350 g spaghetti*
salt and black pepper	*salt and black pepper*
6 tablespoons corn oil	*6 tablespoons corn oil*
2 large cloves garlic	*2 large cloves garlic*
3 tablespoons chopped parsley	*3 tablespoons chopped parsley*

SPICED MEATBALLS

3 tablespoons corn oil	*3 tablespoons corn oil*
1 medium onion (4 oz)	*1 medium onion (120 g)*
1 lb minced beef	*500 g minced beef*
1 teaspoon salt	*1 teaspoon salt*
black pepper	*black pepper*

½ teaspoon cumin seeds	*½ teaspoon cumin seeds*
½ teaspoon ground coriander	*½ teaspoon ground coriander*
1 egg yolk	*1 egg yolk*
2 oz pine kernels	*50 g pine kernels*
2 oz sultanas	*50 g sultanas*

SWEET AND SOUR CHINESE CABBAGE

1 lb Chinese cabbage	*500 g Chinese cabbage*
1 teaspoon salt	*1 teaspoon salt*
3 teaspoons sugar	*3 teaspoons sugar*
2 tablespoons vinegar	*2 tablespoons vinegar*
2 tablespoons corn oil	*2 tablespoons corn oil*
soya sauce	*soya sauce*

1. Put a large pan of salted water to boil for the spaghetti.
2. Heat 1 tablespoon oil for the meatballs in a large frying pan. Chop the onion finely and fry gently for 5 minutes.
3. Place the minced beef in a bowl with the salt, black pepper to taste, cumin seeds and coriander. Add the onion, egg yolk, pine kernels and sultanas and mix well, adjusting the seasoning to taste.
4. Place the corn oil for the spaghetti in a small saucepan. Crush the garlic with a little salt. Chop the parsley. Add both to the oil and place over a very low heat. The garlic must not brown.
5. Divide the meat mixture into four. Flour the hands and divide each quarter into 4 small pieces, rolling into balls. Add the spaghetti to the boiling water and cook for 12 minutes. Heat the remaining 2 tablespoons oil in the frying pan, and fry the 16 meatballs for about 10 minutes, turning to brown all sides. Heat two serving dishes
6. Meanwhile, shred the cabbage thinly. Place the salt in a teacup with the sugar and vinegar. Heat the oil in a large saucepan and add the cabbage. Stir until well mixed with the oil. Sprinkle with a few drops of soya sauce and pour in the vinegar mixture. Cook, uncovered, over a high heat for no more than 2 minutes. The cabbage should be very crisp.
7. Drain the spaghetti, divide between 4 plates and pour the garlic sauce over each. Place the meatballs and the cabbage in the warmed dishes and keep hot while eating the first course.

Curried Tomato Soup (page 3)
made in advance or from the freezer
Orange Glazed Ham with Noodles (page 154)
Whole Beans with Almonds
(version of broccoli page 93)
Instant Banana Cream (page 165)

ORANGE GLAZED HAM WITH NOODLES

4 slices gammon, ½ inch thick	*4 slices gammon, 1 cm thick*
12 oz noodles	*350 g noodles*
salt	*salt*
1 orange	*1 orange*
1 oz soft brown sugar	*30 g soft brown sugar*

WHOLE BEANS WITH ALMONDS

1 lb frozen whole green beans	*500 g frozen whole green beans*
salt	*salt*
1 oz butter	*25 g butter*
2 oz whole blanched almonds	*50 g whole blanched almonds*
black pepper	*black pepper*

INSTANT BANANA CREAM

2 bananas	*2 bananas*
2 teaspoons rum	*2 teaspoons rum*
10 fl oz whipping cream	*¼ litre whipping cream*
2 teaspoons caster sugar	*2 teaspoons caster sugar*
1 oz roasted hazelnuts	*25 g roasted hazelnuts*

1. Put a large pan of water on for the noodles.
2. Skin the bananas and place in a blender or processor with the rum. Blend until completely puréed. Meanwhile, whip the cream

with the sugar until thick. Pour the banana mixture onto the cream, whisk in and pile into 4 individual glasses. Sprinkle with hazelnuts and chill until required.

3. Heat the grill and put serving dishes to warm. Place the ham under the grill and cook under a medium heat for 5 minutes.

4. Heat 1 inch (2 cm) depth of water in a saucepan for the beans. Add the beans when boiling with ½ teaspoon salt and simmer for 3–5 minutes until just tender.

5. Put the noodles into the other pan of boiling water with 1 teaspoon salt. Simmer for 5–8 minutes until tender.

6. Grate the orange rind and squeeze the juice. Place the sugar in a small saucepan, add the rind and a little juice. Heat until the sugar is melted, adding enough juice to make a thick syrupy mixture.

7. Turn the ham, spread with the syrup mixture and cook for a further 3–5 minutes until the sugar caramelizes.

8. Drain the beans. Heat the butter in the same pan, add the almonds and cook in the butter until golden. Return the beans to the pan and turn in the buttery mixture. Sprinkle with black pepper.

9. Drain the noodles. Keep these, the ham and the beans warm in the serving dishes while drinking the soup.

SUGGESTED MENU COMBINATIONS
(WITH NO TIME LIMITATION)

1. Avocado Soup (page 2)
   Sautéed Veal with Caraway Noodles (page 56)
   Vegetable Medley (page 100)
   Blackberry Brulée (page 168)

2. Beans Niçoise (page 104)
   Brandied Pork with Noodles (page 63)
   Carrots with Cardamom (page 95)
   Hot Grapefruit Soufflé (page 131)

3. Celeriac Remoulade (page 106)
   Chillied Chicken Livers with Rice (page 51)
   Buttered Leeks (page 98)
   Instant Cheesecake (page 167)

4. Aubergines with Tomato Sauce (page 138)
   Lamb with Celery and Rice (page 69)
   Zabaglione (page 159)

5. Taramasalata (page 22)
   Meatballs in Tomato Sauce with Noodles (page 59)
   Green Salad
   Apple Snow (page 130)

6. Tagliatelle with Smoked Salmon (page 82)
   Turkey in Red Wine (page 55)
   Sprouts with Brazil Nuts (page 99)
   Grapefruit and Mint Sorbet (page 173)

INDEX